The Ten Lost Tribes:

A People of Destiny

The Ten Lost Tribes:

A People of Destiny

**An Account of
Assyrian Conquest
and
Israelite Captivity**

by

Clay McConkie, Ph.D.

BONNEVILLE BOOKS ™
Springville, Utah

ISBN: 1-55517-587-2
v.1

Published by Bonneville Books
an imprint of Cedar Fort, Inc.
925 N. Main Springville, UT, 84663
www.cedarfort.com

Distributed by:

Typeset by Marny K. Parkin
Cover design by Adam Ford
Cover design © 2001 by Lyle Mortimer
Printed in the United States of America
10 9 8 7 6 5 4 3 2 1
Printed on acid-free paper

 Library of Congress Cataloging-in-Publication Data
McConkie, Clay.
 The ten lost tribes : a people of destiny : an account of the Assyrian conquest and Israelite captivity / by Clay McConkie.
     p. cm.
Includes bibliographical references.
 ISBN 1-55517-587-2 (pbk. : alk. paper)
1. Lost tribes of Israel. 2. Church of Jesus Christ of Latter-day Saints--Doctrines. I. Title.
 BX8643.L66 M33 2002
 289.3'2--dc21
                              2001006244

CONTENTS

PREFACE

Somewhere in the confines of the earth, at a place traditionally associated with the *land of the north,* the lost tribes of Israel exist as a nation. They are very possibly not intermingled among the different countries of the world, as some might suppose, but are living as a separate group of people at an undisclosed location.

Unlike in times past, little is said about them anymore, and on occasion when the subject of their return is mentioned, it is almost regarded as fiction. Yet in the future when the rumor comes that crumbling rock and ice have opened up a passageway in the *north countries* and a mysterious highway has appeared, then people will know that the ten tribes are finally on their way!

The Four Wives
and the Twelve Sons of Jacob
of the House of Israel

Leah

1. Reuben
2. Simeon
3. Levi
4. Judah

Bilhah

5. Dan
6. Naphtali

Zilpah

7. Gad
8. Asher

Leah

9. Issachar
10. Zebulun

Rachel

11. Joseph
12. Benjamin

THE DIVISION OF THE TRIBES

Kingdom of Israel

1. Reuben
2. Simeon
3. Dan
4. Naphtali
5. Gad
6. Asher
7. Issachar
8. Zebulun
9. *Ephraim*
10. *Manasseh*
11. Benjamin (part)

Kingdom of Judah

1. Judah
2. Levi
3. Benjamin (part)

Kings of Israel and Judah

Kingdom of Israel	Kingdom of Judah
Jeroboam I	Rehoboam
Nadab	Abijam
Baasha	Asa
Elah	Jehoshaphat
Zimri	Jehoram
Omri	Ahaziah
Ahab	Athaliah
Ahaziah	Joash
Jehoram	Amaziah
Jehu	Uzziah
Jehoahaz	Jotham
Jehoash	Ahaz
Jeroboam II	Hezekiah
Zachariah	Manasseh
Shallum	Amon
Menahem	Josiah
Pekahiah	Jehoahaz
Pekah	Jehoiakim
Hoshea	Jehoiachin
	Zedekiah

Nineteen Kings   **Twenty Kings**
c. 930–721 B.C.   c. 930–587 B.C.

A New Millennium

As the world approached the calendar year of 2000, there were sundry predictions that this finally might be the time for the second coming of Jesus Christ. Depending upon the accuracy of chronology, the idea was that at the beginning of this particular time period, whenever it turned out to be, the important event might occur.

Such speculation was based partly on the Book of Revelation in the Bible where it speaks of a record bound with seven seals, each seal allegedly representing a period in world history of one thousand years. Since the time of Adam and Eve in the Garden of Eden, in other words, the year 2000 would signal the end of six millennia, and the beginning of the millennium to follow would consequently be the occasion of the Second Coming.

Although the Bible states that no one but God knows the exact date for this latter event, not even "the angels of heaven," still it was significant at the time to know that one millennium was coming to an end and another one beginning, thinking also that something might possibly happen at this specific point in history. And yet one of the problems involved was trying to determine the correct status of the calendar.

Prior to the year 2000, people throughout the world enthusiastically celebrated the approach of a new

1

millennium, and when it supposedly occurred, there were additional celebrations. But according to the calendar, all of this was accomplished one year too early, since a new century or millennium always begins with an odd number. This means that the year 2000 was actually the end of the old millennium and 2001 the beginning of the new.

Proof of this is seen by viewing the first century A.D. as comprising one hundred years, 1 through 100, with the second century beginning with the year 101.

1 to 100	First Century
101 to 200	Second Century
201 to 300	Third Century

Progressing down through the centuries, the nineteenth to twenty-first centuries would then appear as follows:

1801 to 1900	Nineteenth Century
1901 to 2000	Twentieth Century
2001 to 2100	Twenty-first Century

Yet as far as the 2000 celebrations are concerned, those who said that the twenty-first century and new millennium began at an earlier time could be right after all. There is the possibility, for example, that centuries ago an error was made in calculating chronology which placed the present calendar at a point that is at least three or four years behind schedule. An instance of this is that biblical scholars often set the birth of Jesus Christ at about 3 or 4 B.C., or even before that time, and if this is true, a hypothetical date of 4 B.C. would say that the new century and millennium which theoretically began in 2001 really took place in 1997!

But whatever the correct date, whether before or after the year 2001, the important thing has to do with a much more significant circumstance, the idea that the date marks not only the beginning of a new century and a new millennium but also the commencement of the seventh thousand years of the world's recorded history. According to the record known as *The Doctrine and Covenants*, a book of scripture endorsed by the Mormon Church, this would be comparable to the opening of the seventh seal referred to in the eighth chapter of the Book of Revelation, the other six seals being the thousand year periods preceding it.

"The first seal contains the things of the first thousand years," the record says, "and the second also of the second thousand years, and so on until the seventh." All of these together pertain to "the revealed will, mysteries, and works of God; the hidden things of his economy concerning this earth during the seven thousand years of its continuance, or its temporal existence."

The Doctrine and Covenants further states that sometime in the beginning of the seventh thousand years, there will be a final countdown of latter-day occurrences in preparation for the second coming of Jesus Christ. This will be in connection with the seven angels and trumpets mentioned in the seventh seal.

> And the sounding of the trumpets of the seven angels is the preparing and finishing of his work in the beginning of the seventh thousand years, the preparing of the way before the time of his coming.[1]

Certainly these are remarkable statements and interpretations, both in phrasing and intended meaning. They constitute an important adjunct to the material contained in the Book of Revelation. And the thing that makes them extremely compelling as a subject is that the period of time involved is *now*, sometime at the beginning of the

3

new millennium and during the commencement of the seventh thousand years!

At the same time, it is significant that the millennium generally referred to is one whose spelling is in lower case and without a capital. It is the one signifying the final one thousand years of the earth's temporal existence, during the course of which, very possibly during the early part of the twenty-first century, the biblical Millennium will begin. This second era, previewed by prophets all down through time, is to be ushered in when the Lord returns and will be accompanied by worldwide physical changes including the burning of the earth by fire!

Problems of Chronology

In the fifth chapter of the Book of Revelation, it refers to a record that was sealed with seven seals which according to the Doctrine and Covenants contained "the revealed will, mysteries, and works of God." In further detail, it included "the hidden things of his economy concerning this earth during the seven thousand years of its continuance, or its temporal existence."

By this interpretation, each seal designates a millennium of world history, starting with the time of Adam and Eve in the garden of Eden and continuing into the present. It is also here where it says that in the beginning of the seventh thousand years, the Lord will begin making final preparations prior to his Second Coming.

A significant problem, however, is reconciling the chronology in the Bible with that contained in the Doctrine and Covenants. For example, in the Book of Revelation regarding the 6th seal, it states that the heavens will depart as a scroll and every mountain and island will be moved out of its place. This is to be followed by the opening of the seventh seal, or the beginning of the seventh thousand years, after which there will be silence in heaven for about the space of half an hour.[2]

But in the Doctrine and Covenants, the phenomena of the scroll in heaven and by implication the moving of mountains and islands from their places both occur during the period of time *after* the one-half hour of silence instead of *before*.[3] And what this amounts to is not only a chronological problem but also the possibility that some of the material relating to the sixth seal in the Book of Revelation, if not all or most of it, pertains not to the sixth thousand years of world history at all but rather to the seventh!

A strategic factor in the situation is the reference to the *one-half hour of silence in heaven.* In relation to heaven's reckoning of time, which is "one day is with the Lord as a thousand years," this would amount to approximately twenty-one years, considerable time for many things to happen.[4] In both the Bible and the Doctrine and Covenants, in fact, this period of time could possibly be interpreted, at least in part, as the interval prior to when the Lord will complete the final phase of "the preparing and finishing of his work in the beginning of the seventh thousand years, the preparing of the way before the time of his coming."

Certain events definitely need to occur, however, before the start of the biblical Millennium mentioned in scripture, and because of this it is probably well not to watch the calendar too closely but rather be more concerned about the *signs of the times.* They are the things that will dictate what happens, rather than any study of timetables or chronology. At the same time, it is important to be well acquainted with such signs, and the following items in theoretical sequence show briefly what they are. The main question pertains to the people known as the *lost tribes of Israel,* whether their return will be before the Millennium or after.

1. Opening of seventh seal and beginning of seventh millennium.

2. A one half-hour of silence in heaven.

3. The seven angels with trumpets.

4. Increase in church activity, including temple building and missionary work.

5. Meeting at Adam-ondi-Ahman.

6. Construction of a city and temple in Zion.

7. Reconstruction of the city and temple in Jerusalem.

8. *Return of the lost tribes of Israel.*

9. A gigantic earthquake.

10. Sun, moon, and stars phenomena.

11. Oceans and seas going beyond their bounds.

12. Sign of the Son of Man.

13. Beginning of final plagues and the Battle of Armageddon.

14. Curtain of heaven unfolded.

15. Mountains and islands moving out of their places.

16. Appearances of Jesus Christ.

    a. Mount of Olives

    b. waters of the great deep

    c. islands of the sea

    d. Mount Zion in America

Surely the final segment of the last days will be a dramatic presentation and culmination of spectacular events. It will be the grand finale to more than six thousand years of the world's recorded history and the passage of mankind into a new era of temporal existence. Also at the point when this finally happens, there will be a new heaven and a new earth, and those remaining on the planet will herald the beginning of the predicted Millennium and one thousand years of world peace and prosperity!

But again there are many events still to occur before the end comes, and an important question is whether or not the sixth millennium has actually ended and the seventh one begun. There is also the question of whether events assigned to the sixth seal, as recorded in the Bible, pertain to the sixth thousand years of time or more accurately to the seventh thousand years that follow it. These latter occurrences include (1) a large earthquake, (2) the sun, moon, and stars phenomena, (3) the opening of heaven like a scroll, and (4) mountains and islands moving out of their places, all of which are of extraordinary magnitude and would definitely appear to belong to the later period.

There are those, however, who might say that ample quakes of high intensity have already taken place in partial fulfillment of the sixth seal, the same being true with unusual circumstances pertaining to the sky. As a result of modern industry and air pollution, there have been times when both the sun and the moon were unusually reddened or darkened, and also occasions where meteoric showers and astral illusions during earthquakes could be viewed as falling or reeling stars.

And yet the pointed references in ancient and modern scripture to irregular occurrences in the sky during the last days appear to be much more than any of these. Rather they would say that when the actual signs are given, they will occasion immediate response and establish the fact that such things have never happened before. There are miraculous events yet to come, in other words, and at the present stage of things and in a modern-day world characterized by revolutionary changes, some of them could take place very quickly.

Also in relation to the sixth seal, the two occurrences pertaining to the *opening of heaven like a scroll* and the *moving of mountains and islands from their places* should both be listed in the seal which follows, the place where they obviously belong. This in turn suggests that there might have been translation errors in the Bible and that the large earthquake and astronomical occurrences were meant to be included in the latter seal as well.

Consequently, the actual conditions of the sixth seal, referring to the sixth thousand years of time, might more accurately be represented by the following: (1) widespread earthquakes, (2) wars and rumors of wars, (3) famines and pestilence, and (4) the preaching of the gospel throughout the world, all of which are cited in the 24th chapter of Matthew as characteristics of the last days. In addition, major events such as Genghis Khan conquering Asia and killing more than five million people, the bubonic plague in the fourteenth century taking another twenty-four million, and the regime of Nazi Germany executing six million Jews during World War II are all types of atrocity and pestilence that might be representative of things pertaining to the sixth seal.

Certainly there are problems in the Book of Revelation, including those relative to chronology, which have not yet been solved. Their resolution for the time being appears to be unlikely and is something evidently reserved for the future. But in the meantime, with information gained from both ancient and modern scripture, a tentative but reasonable view of a very puzzling situation can still be obtained!

Signs of the Times

If the seventh millennium has already begun, depending on the correctness of the calendar, it puts an extremely important emphasis on the present period of time. It means that the signal has already been given, in other words, or soon will be, for the *preparing and finishing* of the work that needs to be done before the Second Coming of Christ.

Much has taken place previously, especially during the last two centuries, but the implication of the *beginning of the seventh thousand years* is that now the process of things will be accelerated. Once the lower case millennium begins, the upper case Millennium will soon follow. And what makes all of this compelling and relevant is that the preparatory work might very possibly be completed in the early part of the twenty-first century!

Certain crucial events outlined in prophecy and scripture must still occur, however, but because they are relatively few in number, the idea that things might happen very quickly in an ultramodern age is definitely a possibility.

(1) One of these events will be an extraordinary meeting to be held in the valley known as Adam-ondi-Ahman. The time involved is sometime prior to the Second Coming, and in attendance will be an almost unbelievable group of dignitaries accompanied by appointed guests.

Adam himself is scheduled to conduct this meeting, and all of the principle figures who have held priesthood keys in the various dispensations down through history will be present. At that time they will report on their respective stewardships and deliver up their keys to Adam. Enoch, Noah, Abraham, Moses, and the latter-day prophet Joseph Smith will all take part, and at the designated time the presiding officer Jesus Christ will then appear and receive from Adam the various keys and stewardships.

(2) Also before the Second Advent and the beginning of the Millennium, construction of two important temples will take place, one in the central part of America and the other in Jerusalem. Information pertaining to the first of these, which will be built as part of the City of Zion, is well documented, but that relating to the second is still relatively unknown.

For one thing, it is unclear as to who will actually build the Jerusalem temple, whether members of the Mormon Church, which is currently building temples throughout the world, or the Jewish people themselves. The temple site also remains undisclosed, the traditional spot being on the Temple Mount but with the possibility that the temple itself might be at some other location.

In either of these two cases, it is certain that both groups have the subject on their minds. Jewish preparations are well under way in regard to temple plans and equipment, and attempts have even been made to lay a cornerstone. As for the Mormon Church, it has made no official declaration about any temple to be built in Jerusalem.

(3) At about the same time that the temple is constructed in Zion, the building of the city itself will be commenced. This will then continue into the Millennium. As for Jerusalem, the prophecies are that it will undergo a rebuilding program, eventually becoming along with Zion one of the two religious capitals of the world.

"For out of Zion shall go forth the law," the scripture says, "and the word of the Lord from Jerusalem."[5]

These particular events, therefore, the meeting at Adam-ondi-Ahman and the construction relative to the two cities and temples, are among the most obvious that need to occur before the Millennium, all of which could happen quickly in today's society. Yet there are still three other events, although probably not so imminent, that will occur toward the end of this same time period, namely a series of plagues and astronomic phenomena, the great battle at Armageddon, and the return from seclusion of the ten lost tribes of Israel!

(4) Toward the end of the last days, for example, there will occur an almost unbelievable sequence of devastating scourges and desolation. In addition to what has already taken place, there will be continuing natural disasters such as storms, floods, fires, winds and earthquakes, accompanied by plagues, disease, and famine. Events and circumstances referred to in the Book of Revelation and the 24th chapter of Matthew, including the sun, moon, and stars phenomena, will become a reality.

The world will experience a spectacular finale, as it were, of astronomic and geologic eruptions, as well as the disastrous plagues associated with the trumpets of the seven angels, all in preparation for a new heaven and a new earth. These in turn will be the final signs of the times that the end is near, as well as a cleansing process to help prepare the world for the approaching Millennium.

(5) But the most devastating event, by far, will be the Battle of Armageddon! Indeed, when the world sees many nations sending men and munitions to the Middle East for the purpose of annihilating Israel, this is the time when people will know that the end of the world is imminent. After all of the other signs have been given,

this one last event will set a more exact time and place for the grand denouement of human affairs!

Nothing will compare with this last great battle. Although modern warfare and technology will undoubtedly be involved, there are also prophecies that huge armies of horsemen will come equipped with swords and shields. Attention as never before will be focused on the Middle Eastern area. The world will divide itself into two main groups, those supporting the Jewish people in Palestine and those who would destroy them, and not until the end of a life-consuming battle will the outcome be decided.

At that time, according to prophecy, the Lord himself will appear and terminate the fighting. On besieging armies all the way from Megiddo and Esdraelon in the north to Jerusalem in the south he will spread fire, hailstones, and brimstone and quickly bring the invasions to an end. This and other sudden appearances, involving a spectacular incident at the Mount of Olives and the dispersal of ocean and seas back into the north countries, will usher in the period of time known as the Millennium, and at this point in the beginning of the seventh thousand years, the much publicized and long-awaited era of peace will finally begin!

(6) Yet in conclusion there is still a sixth event scheduled to take place sometime before or after the Second Coming of Christ. This will be the restoration of the ten tribes of Israel at the time of their return from a long period of absence and concealment. Whether their reappearance will actually occur prior to the Battle of Armageddon or after is unknown, but in any case the tribes will be coming from somewhere in the north country, eventually arriving at the temple located in the City of Zion. There they will be welcomed by other Israelites and will receive at their hands an important religious

endowment. Also they will bring with them certain "rich treasures," including possibly their records which undoubtedly will give important evidence and information pertaining to over two millennia of personal history.

Certainly the return of these tribes will be one of the most unusual occurrences of the last days. Never before in the accounts of the Bible has there been a subject more unorthodox and unique. The circumstances of their disappearance in the sixth or seventh century B.C. and the succeeding period of complete seclusion definitely set them apart as an important reality to be reckoned with, both as to their sojourn as a lost civilization and also the very purpose of their existence.

When the truth about them is fully known, in fact, it will undoubtedly answer many puzzling questions, not only about the tribes themselves as a people but the earth and human family in general!

The Final Events

Along with the various geologic and astronomic phenomena that have been predicted for the last days, there is also the small cluster of events in particular that will be occurring at about the same time, all in the beginning of the seventh millennium. A more detailed description of these occurrences, the first of which is the important meeting to be held in a valley in northwestern Missouri, gives added meaning to this extraordinary period of history.

Adam-ondi-Ahman

It is uncertain as to how many people will be attending the conference at Adam-ondi-Ahman. The geographic area involved is large enough to accommodate an extremely large congregation, but at the same time, those participating will be there by appointment or invitation only. An important aspect of the event is that it will be a very private one, experienced in person by relatively few people. It will come and go unnoticed, in other words, except for those who are entitled and privileged to be there.

The meeting will be a sequel to one that took place approximately five thousand years ago when Adam met with seven generations of his posterity in the same valley, giving them his final blessing and also receiving a visitation from Jesus Christ. Indeed, this second meeting will be its historic namesake, an event taking place not too long before the beginning of the Millennium.

To those in attendance it will definitely be a signal that the Lord's second advent is imminent, that everything is on schedule, and that certain catastrophic occurrences lie just ahead. It will be one of the final signs that the seventh thousand years of the earth's temporal existence is well under way and that the earth very soon will be plagued with a series of devastations and then burned with fire!

City and Temple of Zion

Unlike the meeting at Adam-ondi-Ahman, the building of a city and temple in the *center place of Zion* will be an announcement to a much larger number of people that the end of an era is definitely drawing to a close. When the necessary arrangements are completed and construction of the various edifices actually begins, it will be a significant time of faith building and religious confirmation, and many will be called to participate in the unusual activities centering in western Missouri.

As to the building of the temple itself, the project will be a continuation of a vast program of temple construction already in progress, albeit on a much larger scale. The temple in Zion, in fact, will not be just one building but twenty-four, according to the original plan, a large temple complex occupying two enlarged city blocks fifteen acres each.

The twenty-four individual temples have also been described as rooms or compartments, "all joined together in a circular form and arched over the center." But the idea in the beginning appears rather to have been separate structures. According to a plan submitted by Joseph Smith in 1833, there were to be twelve temples on each block, situated alternately in rows of three. The first of these buildings, being eighty-seven feet long and sixty-one feet wide, was to be built near the center of the first block.

In any case, the preliminary plan has been in existence for well over one hundred and fifty years, and when the time comes for its implementation, or one similar to it, the actual construction of the central portion of Zion and its environs could occur very quickly!

This location will then become the scene of many significant events immediately preceding and following the Second Coming and the Millennium, one of them being the arrival of the ten tribes of Israel from the land of the north. Another will be a historic meeting of Jesus Christ with 144,000 missionaries, twelve thousand from each tribe, who will be involved in a worldwide program of missionary work.

Then in addition to this will be other unusual events and circumstances pertaining to the city and temple. Animal sacrifices, for example, non-existent as a Christian practice since the Meridian of Time, will be reinstated as part of the restitution of all things and will again become an important religious principle and ordinance. This will not be just a temporary restoration but a continuing aspect of the gospel.

Also it has been alleged that the religious records hidden in the original hill Cumorah, said by some to be located in Central America, will eventually be retrieved and redeposited in the new temple in Zion. All of the plates that the prophet Mormon first placed in the hill called Shim and later transferred to Cumorah will finally be relocated in a permanent repository.

Indeed, such conditions and events will be an interesting and significant part of the world's recorded history, as well as a fitting inaugural for the newly-built City of Zion, also known as the New Jerusalem.

The Temple in Old Jerusalem

One of the specific prophecies which has been made concerning Jerusalem of old, the historic city in Palestine, is that it will be rebuilt prior to the Millennium and that the ancient temple will be reconstructed. Although much of the city's renewal has apparently already taken place, the monumental task that remains, of course, and the thing that presents potential difficulties, is the rebuilding of the temple. This is a project surrounded at present by uncertain circumstances. And whether the construction is to be accomplished by members of the Mormon Church, most of whom are reputed to be of the tribe of Ephraim, or by the Jewish people themselves, who are descended from Judah, remains to be seen.

If the temple is built by those of the tribe of Judah, an almost insurmountable problem might be the building's location. This is because the Jewish people in Jerusalem insist that it be at the original site on the Temple Mount, the place where the Dome of the Rock now stands, or at least very close to it. Yet any attempt to interfere with this particular Islamic shrine would be tantamount to open rebellion and warfare, a potentiality that already exists between Israel and the Palestinians.

In this connection, however, there is a certain possibility that might allow for a compromise between the two groups. It is the idea that someday in the future the historic Dome and the reconstruction of Herod's Temple, as the original temple was called, could both be accommodated on the Temple Mount.

If the theory of a certain professor at Hebrew University in Jerusalem is correct, it means that the location of the earlier temple was *not* on the present site of the Dome of the Rock, as commonly believed, but some eighty-five feet to the north. This would allow a new temple to be built at the exact location by either Jews or Christians without seriously disrupting any religious worship of the Moslems. And even if all of these calculations prove to be incorrect, it still might be that a fourth temple, following those of Solomon, Zerubbabel, and Herod, could ultimately be built at some other place.

It might be, in fact, that a temple constructed in Jerusalem by people descended from Ephraim, during the same general time period as the temple in Zion, could be at an entirely new location, even on the Mount of Olives across from the city proper. A precedent for this kind of situation exists today in the history of Brigham Young University in Provo, Utah.

In this particular instance, the so-called Temple Hill on which the university is located was so named because its founder Brigham Young reportedly said that a temple would one day be built there. But when a temple was eventually constructed, the site was at the mouth of a canyon a short distance to the northeast. And although this entire area is technically on the hill which is part of the alluvial fan or plateau on which the campus is situated, the canyon site is still probably not the location for the temple that most people had in mind.

The point is that tradition often regards things as having to be a certain way, yet when the time comes for reality to take place, something quite different might occur. If the temple in Jerusalem is to be built on the Temple Mount, for example, it appears that there might be a logical way for it to be achieved. But on the other hand, if it has to be done at another location nearby, that also is a possibility. The important thing is that not too far in the future, there will definitely be a Jerusalem temple, and according to religious prophecy it will have to be completed and in operation before the Second Coming of Jesus Christ!

Final Calamities and Armageddon

By far, the most serious aspect of the last days will be the devastating calamities predicted in the Book of Revelation, all part of the opening of the seventh seal. This will include not only a series of natural disasters but also famine, plague, and disease, accompanied at the very end by what is predicted to be the greatest battle of the ages, the one referred to in scripture as Armageddon.

At the time of this last great battle, as outlined in the Bible, the forces of Gog will come down from the north country out of the land called Magog, which traditionally is the same as ancient Scythia near the upper parts of the Black and Caspian Seas. In a modern world known for its high technology and scientific achievement, the invaders will appear as in days of old, "all of them riding upon horses, a great company, and a mighty army."[6]

This will not be just an ordinary invasion. The intent of the aggressor will be to conquer Israel and destroy it! The bitterness and hatred for the Jewish people, after building up in the Middle East for centuries, will suddenly break loose in a huge onslaught of mounted warriors. From many nations in different parts of the world, including ancient Persia or Iran, and also Libya and Ethiopia, they will gather around Gog their leader, "all of them clothed with all sorts of armor, even a great company with bucklers and shields, all of them handling swords."[7] And in one gigantic thrust, the invading armies will cover the land like a cloud.

According to the prophet Joel, it will be a time of great trouble, "a day of darkness and of gloominess, a day of clouds and of thick darkness." "A fire devoureth before them," he says, "and behind them a flame burneth: the land is as the garden of Eden before them, and behind them a desolate wilderness; yea, and nothing shall escape them."[8]

But all of this will be for naught as far as Gog and his forces are concerned. Eventually the Lord himself will intervene, and with a rain of hailstones, fire, and brimstone he will bring the devastating invasions to an end. A countless number of men and animals will fall on that fateful day, and their dead bodies will cover the open fields.

Especially in Jerusalem to the south there will be a dramatic end to the battle. After being overrun by enemy forces, and at a time when everything appears to be lost, the Jewish people will be delivered in a spectacular and supernatural manner as the Lord himself appears and stands upon the Mount of Olives across from the city.

At that moment, according to the book of Zechariah, the mount will cleave in two, one part shifting to the north and the other to the south, providing a miraculous pathway of escape. The captives will flee to "the valley of the mountains," and much like the parting of the Red Sea when Moses led the Hebrews out of Egypt, a cataclysmic separation of land will now save a similar group, the embattled inhabitants of Jerusalem and the modern-day descendants of ancient Israel.

This one occurrence, apart from everything else, is the single one that stands out during the Battle of Armageddon. It is the surprising climax which will bring all fighting and aggression to an end. It is also the event, among several others, that will announce the Second Coming of Jesus Christ and signal the beginning of the long-awaited Millennium.

Surely all of this will be a dramatic conclusion, and in many ways a tragic one, to more than six thousand years of the world's recorded history. Never before has anything of such magnitude taken place. Also the momentous occurrences which follow, including widespread burning over the face of the earth, will be the termination of telestial life, the time referred to in prophecy and scripture as the *end of the world.*

And yet there is still one more event, occurring either before or after the Lord's Second Coming, that will play an extremely important part in this final drama. In some ways less sensational, compared to some of the incidents surrounding it, yet extraordinary and phenomenal in others, it is an occurrence that stands noticeably apart from all of the rest. This is the predicted return of the ten lost tribes of Israel!

Restoration of the Ten Tribes

There are very few subjects pertaining to this time period that are more unusual and important than the return of the lost tribes. Because of the particular circumstances involved, this one event especially invites a very different kind of attention.

First there is the matter of their mysterious disappearance in the north country following years of Assyrian captivity. Second is the prediction that their eventual return from an unknown place will be accompanied by unusual phenomena pertaining to *rock, ice, and water.* At the time of their reappearance, in fact, it is said that prophets among them will actually "smite the rocks, and the ice shall flow down at their presence," after which a *highway* will be raised up in order to provide passage over some part of a sea or ocean.

An opposing view, of course, is that the tribes are really not lost at all in the usual sense but are presently intermingled and scattered among different countries of the world. In other words, they are part of the prophecy which states that the house of Israel is to be sifted "among all nations, like as corn is sifted in a sieve."[9]

And yet there are those who would definitely interpret the scriptures more definitively, maintaining that this particular group of Israelites, for some unknown reason or purpose, has remained intact over the centuries and will someday reappear just as mysteriously as they once disappeared!

This kind of theory obviously implies that the ten tribes are geographically in a very unorthodox place, which in turn involves certain aspects pertaining to the supernatural. It is obvious, in other words, that such a group does not exist in any of the northern regions which have been explored extensively in all directions, nor is there any definite situation or setting that immediately might be associated with the exotic phenomena of rock, ice, and water.

Certainly the appellation *of lost tribes* given to this elusive civilization of people is more than just a unique name or title. The term rather is one with extraordinary implications. Not only does it suggest a group inaccessible and remote from all others, but at the same time one that someday will be restored to normal society in a remarkable manner. Indeed, it has been predicted that the ten tribes will eventually return and once more become a visible part of the House of Israel.

The main questions are *when*, and under *what kind* of circumstances. Also *where* will the people be coming from, and *why* were they segregated from world society in the first place? Why was it necessary to scatter one segment of Israel throughout the nations but relegate another, a relatively small one, to some remote and nondescript part of the globe?

Undoubtedly these are questions that prompt many different kinds of answers, and people might well tire of them sometimes and prefer to leave them alone. Often they regard them as mysteries and consequently set them aside in preference to subjects less controversial.

But the questions are always there, and especially as time draws closer for the final religious prophecies to be fulfilled and the historic Millennium to occur, it becomes even more important to be knowledgeable about the signs of the times. Adequate preparation for what lies ahead, in a way, demands it. Surely if people want to be informed, they will seek interpretations of all that has been revealed in connection with this important time period, which includes not just an awareness of certain events to come, but also of things pertaining specifically to the historic gathering of Israel and the eventual restoration of the ten tribes!

Genesis

During the latter part of the tenth century B.C. following the death of King Solomon, the ten tribes made their first appearance in history as a nation. The occasion was the dramatic division of the House of Israel in which all of the tribes except Judah and one-half of Benjamin broke away and became a political entity by themselves. At that time they were known as the Kingdom of Israel while the remaining group went by the name of Judah.

This left the new nation with a tribal makeup of Reuben, Simeon, Levi, Dan, Naphtali, Gad, Asher, Issachar, Zebulun, Joseph, and Benjamin, each tribe listed according to the age of its leader. Joseph was usually not mentioned as a tribe but was represented in double portion by his two sons Manasseh and Ephraim.

The dissenting number, therefore, not counting Joseph, ended up as eleven and one-half tribes, and when Levi later transferred to the Kingdom of Judah because of religious reasons, the resulting number thereafter was generally regarded as ten.

It was unfortunate that the Israelites ever divided, in the first place, and if things had been handled more astutely after Solomon's death, the schism might have been avoided. And yet the trouble between Israel in the north and Judah in the south had been developing for years, and it was probably inevitable that a separation finally occurred.

In any case, the two kingdoms existed separately for approximately two hundred years until Israel finally succumbed to the forces of the Assyrian Empire between 733 and 721 B.C., the same thing happening to Judah under the Chaldeans of Babylonia a century and a quarter later. At this time, the relationship between these two kindred groups almost completely disappeared.

The history of the Kingdom of Judah during the Babylonian captivity and also the time period which followed is fairly well documented in both biblical and secular sources. But as for the Kingdom of Israel, things are much less apparent. An account of this latter group, in fact, is so obscure in regard to the conquests by Assyria that at least some of the people have often been referred to as the *lost tribes of Israel.*

And yet again there are those who say that these tribes are technically not lost at all but are currently scattered and dispersed among the different countries. They are unidentified because of many centuries of geographic change and intermarriage, yet they nevertheless reside somewhere in the northern areas of the globe and someday will reappear out of obscurity, being led by the leaders of their respective congregations.

Even a general location of this mysterious group of people, however, still continues to be a puzzling question, and were it not for a significant amount of evidence to the contrary, it would be easy to accept the view that the ten tribes are indeed in a normal situation somewhere and will eventually come out of modern society in a conventional way. But an alternative viewpoint does exist, as well as a caution, and to accept any explanation that is too ordinary and simplified might well be bypassing the real solution!

Concept of the Tribes

The idea that at least part of the ten tribes are currently dispersed among the nations is actually a true concept. More than half of the original group, in fact, are very probably intermixed not only with people in northern areas but throughout all parts of the world. Yet the important thing is that the other portion, the one that is scheduled to reappear someday in a miraculous manner, is currently residing at a different location. Justification for this view, at least in part, can be found in the conquest and deportation policy of the ancient Assyrian Empire.

It was Assyrian custom, for example, upon conquering a particular area, to deport approximately half of the population and leave the other half where they were, at the same time bringing in colonists from different parts of the empire to take their place. By using such a method the invaders weakened the existing political and social structure of an area and were able to maintain stronger control. An acceptance of this fact is extremely important in understanding the present situation of the ten tribes.

Whereas it is often suggested that the tribes generally were taken en masse into captivity, the more accurate number of captives might have been not even one half but very possibly less. Moreover, it was not a matter of removing whole segments of population without regard to economic, social, or political standing, but rather taking prisoners that might be a threat if left behind, as well as those in the military and the upper classes who could be of more benefit to the empire. As things turned out, it was usually the poorer or lower classes that stayed in the original homeland, people who again were less apt to make trouble politically or who were less skilled in the occupations.

When the ten tribes are viewed in this way, the statement that those who remained in the *south* were part of the group that later was scattered and dispersed throughout different countries is a valid one. The same might even be true of some who were taken captive. But an additional viewpoint, and one that is especially important, is that at least some of those deported to the *north* eventually left their places of captivity in Assyria and disappeared somewhere further into the north country, later to be referred to as the *lost tribes of Israel*.

It is these people, according to religious prophecy, who are waiting for a signal that someday will prompt their return to present-day society. These are the ones spoken of in scripture who will exit through some type of passageway amid falling rock and ice and traverse an improvised highway over an expanse of water. As in times of old when Moses led the children of Israel across the Red Sea, their experience will likewise be a miraculous one involving divine intervention and the supernatural.

All of this, of course, suggests an unusual setting for those who traveled further to the north and entered a place of concealment that would hold them for more than twenty-five centuries. There is definitely an implication of some exotic place or destination. Yet the immediate question, and one that precedes all others, is not so much where these people are presently located but whether or not they are a separate group, distinct and apart from those dispersed among the nations. It is the specific question of existence and correct identity. And once again, the final answer and solution might well be found in the deportation policy of the Assyrian Empire.

If only a certain portion of the tribes was taken into captivity, in other words, serving some unknown purpose as far as biblical history is concerned, it implies very strongly that the people were to remain isolated and apart. It was apparently not meant for them to be involved in any universal dispersion, nor is it likely that they became a hybrid group like those remaining in Palestine. Instead they became part of a dual phenomenon, as it were, consisting of a future *gathering of Israel* on the one hand and the *restoration of the ten tribes* on the other.

In regard to the phenomenon known as the gathering, at least according to one belief, this currently consists of people in many different countries of the world assembling in designated areas and subscribing to the idea that important truths have been restored and a modern Israel is now coming into being. Separate from the Israeli situation in Palestine, the movement comprises a worldwide missionary and training program for the living and a genealogical program for those who are dead. Together these two components constitute much of the latter-day gathering of Israel, the sponsoring institution in this case being the organization known as the Mormon Church.

Also as it turns out, those participating in the movement almost exclusively claim to be related to the tribe of Ephraim. Other Israelite backgrounds are undoubtedly involved, since people from all of the original tribes have been scattered and sifted throughout the nations, but there is still a definite emphasis on this one particular tribe. Even though a person's pedigree might contain lineages from several different groups, along with those that are non-Israelite, it is nevertheless Ephraim that is said to be predominant.

In ancient times this was an important tribe, often

asserting itself beyond the authority of the others, and it was a common occurrence for the Kingdom of Israel as a nation to be called by their name. Consequently, it is not surprising that the descendants of this tribe today are primarily the ones involved in the modern gathering, including not only the membership in general but in particular the leadership.

And the same might also apply to the second part of the dual phenomenon, the return or restoration of the ten tribes. If Ephraim was important anciently, for example, as it is now during the present gathering, it is possible that it will likewise have an important influence among the tribes who are lost, wherever they happen to be located and at what point in time they might return. This would especially be true of the prophets who are leading them.

"And they who are in the north countries," the scripture says, "shall come in remembrance before the Lord; and their prophets shall hear his voice, and shall no longer stay themselves; and they shall smite the rocks, and the ice shall flow down at their presence. And an highway shall be cast up in the midst of the great deep."[10]

Certainly it is logical that the leadership of the lost tribes, those who will be guiding the people back to the mainstream of society, could also be descendants of Ephraim. Again this is the tribe that has been an acknowledged and recognized group from the beginning. Originally it was Ephraim who was set apart and given preferential status by his grandfather Jacob and who ultimately received the main part of the Israelite birthright, and when the tribes return from their long stay of seclusion, it is not inconsistent to believe that some of his descendants at that time will be those who are in authority leading the way.

Much of the gathering, therefore, especially the

prominence of Ephraim and the return of the lost tribes, has a direct relationship to the past and to the ancient conquests of Assyria. The latter in particular forms an important episode in the affairs of the House of Israel. The invasions which took place in Transjordan and Palestine toward the end of the eighth century B.C. were devastating and disruptive, yet at the same time instrumental in preparing the way for an extraordinary period of history. For those who resided in the northern kingdom, it was the beginning of an entirely new era. Not only were people scattered and dispersed in many different directions, but a small and significant part of them was destined eventually to disappear from society completely and for the next twenty-five hundred years remain a strange enigma and mystery!

Assyrian Invasions

In regard to the ten tribes and their subjugation by the Assyrian Empire, it is easy to get the idea that the people generally were taken en masse into captivity. There might have been a few of them left, in other words, but only scattered groups and remnants.

An example of this is the account in the Bible of colonists brought in from Babylon and other parts of the empire to replace those who had been take captive in Samaria, the capital of the Kingdom of Israel. On one occasion the new settlers complained to the Assyrian king that they were being threatened by lions, which might suggest that the area had earlier been denuded of population. The people believed that wild animals had been sent by the Israelite god with whom they were unfamiliar.

In reply the king dispatched one of the captive priests to the area, the purpose being to instruct the people in certain religious matters that might benefit them and help improve their situation. The idea of the priest returning, therefore, along with the threat of incoming lions again might give the impression that the earlier inhabitants had mostly been evacuated.

This is also true in the biblical accounts from 2 Kings and 1 Chronicles which imply that most of the population in the Kingdom of Israel was taken captive.[11] In addition, there is a statement by the prophet Jeremiah following the invasions that "the whole seed of Ephraim" had been cast out.[12]

And yet this type of material and information does not present a picture that is historically correct. It might be that isolated instances such as the lions did occur, but in general the system of only partial deportation by the Assyrian government and corresponding replacement with outsiders is much more likely. Obviously, following the invasions there were adverse circumstances, but the implication that the homeland of the ten tribes was reoccupied by a completely new group of people is unjustified.

Also it was not just in Israel but in other Middle Eastern areas that the Assyrian type of deportation was put into effect. Previously it had been employed by Egyptians, Hittites, and Mesopotamians, and whereas it was also used in Assyria by some of the earlier rulers, it was during the time of Tiglath-Pileser III that it became more prominent and widespread. He was also the one, according to the Bible, who was the first to oppress the Israelite tribes in Palestine.

The conquest of the Kingdom of Israel, in fact, involved not one but three successive Assyrian kings who conducted two separate invasions. The first of these attacks occurred in approximately 733 B.C. when Tiglath-Pileser entered northern Palestine and the area of Transjordan, subjugating a number of cities and taking prisoners.

"In the days of Pekah, king of Israel, came Tiglath-Pileser, king of Assyria, and took Ijon, and Abelbeth-maachah, and Janoah, and Kedesh, and Hazor, and Gilead, and Galilee, all the land of Naphtali, and carried them captive to Assyria." In addition, these conquered regions contained people from the tribes of Asher, Zebulun, Issachar and Dan.

Also across the Jordan River, "he carried them away, even the Reubenites, and the Gadites, and half the tribe of Manasseh, and brought them unto Halah, and Habor, and Hara, and to the river Gozan, unto this day."[13]

The second invasion then commenced in about 724 B.C. when Shalmaneser V attacked Samaria, besieging it three years before taking the city. There is disagreement as to who actually completed this conquest, whether it was the second king or his successor Sargon II, but in either case, the Israelite capital and kingdom finally fell in 721 B.C.

> Then the king of Assyria came up throughout all the land and went up to Samaria and besieged it three years. In the ninth year of Hoshea, the king of Assyria took Samaria, and carried Israel away into Assyria, and placed them in Halah and in Habor by the river Gozan, and in the cities of the Medes.[14]

Obviously much has been deleted or left out of the biblical record in connection with these invasions. The Assyrians were well-known for their warlike nature, for example, and also their brutality, yet no mention is made in the Bible of any atrocities or casualties. Also the number of prisoners claimed by Sargon II, who would have been more apt to overestimate rather than underestimate, was 27,290, much less than what is suggested in the Bible. Moreover, those taken were possibly not removed from the area until two years after the invasion as the Assyrian king returned from a military expedition to Egypt.

The point is that the conquest and subjugation of the ten tribes could have been considerably different from some of the circumstances alluded to in scripture. One thing in particular is that while a large segment of the population was eventually removed, at least an equal number was evidently left behind, later to be scattered and dispersed among the nations. In the former

Kingdom of Israel, these were the people sometimes referred to as *remnants*, located east of the Jordan River as well as throughout northern and central Palestine, and notably in the region of the capital city of Samaria!

The City of Samaria

When the ten tribes were conquered and deported to *Hara, Guzana,* and *Halah,* and also to the *cities of the Medes,* a large part of the tribes still remained in *Transjordan, northern Palestine,* and *Samaria.* This is an important fact to remember and consider. Although the assertion is partly true that the tribes were never really lost, in the first place, but were an identifiable population that was eventually scattered and sifted among the nations, such pertains primarily to those who were left behind, as well as possibly a certain percentage who were taken into captivity.

The Israelites who remained in Transjordan east of the Jordan River, for example, along with those in northern and central Palestine, continued on as they had before. The Bible speaks several times of the *remnants* who were left in these areas and especially those in and around Samaria.

It was Samaria, in fact, that was particularly important and in times past had become almost synonymous with the Kingdom of Israel itself. For more than one hundred and fifty years in this place and city, the people centered their hopes for political freedom and national security. And yet it had not always been this way. Before the time of Samaria, there had been other capital cities, each representing a significant step of development, as well as an unfortunate progress toward division and captivity.

In the beginning, during the time of the first king

Jeroboam, the seat of government had been at Shechem, then later very briefly at Penuel and eventually at Tirzah. Finally in the reign of Omri, Israel's sixth ruler, the permanent capital site was chosen on top of the prominent hill called Samaria.

"And he bought the hill Samaria of Shemer," referring to Omri, "for two talents of silver, and built on the hill, and called the name of the city which he built, after the name of Shemer, owner of the hill, Samaria."[15]

The site in many ways was a very good one. It was centrally located and was favorable in regard to communication and transportation. It is said that the king from his windows could easily see passing ships along the Mediterranean Sea twenty-five miles away. The surrounding countryside was also rich and fertile.

In addition, from a military standpoint the new capital was strategically in an excellent location. The hill could readily be defended, and the higher mountains around it on three sides were far enough away that they could not be used as vantage places by attacking slingers and bowmen.

One of the drawbacks of the site, however, was that it lacked a good water supply. The nearest springs a mile away could easily be cut off during an attack by an invading army. And yet despite this, along with other problems which might have existed, the people of Samaria miraculously held out against the Assyrians for three years during the final siege of the city.[16]

It is almost inconceivable on that occasion that the military forces of Assyria could have been detained so long. Unusual factors and circumstances were undoubtedly involved although they are not mentioned in the Bible. But the city was eventually conquered and sometime later many of its people taken into captivity. The Kingdom of Israel as a political entity tragically came to an end in approximately 721 B.C.

Some eleven years earlier, Tiglath Pileser had made the initial conquest of Israelite territory, establishing Assyrian provinces at Megiddo, Dor on the Mediterranean coast, and Gilead in Transjordan. Now a new province was set up in Samaria, also called *Samarina*, and in all four of these conquered areas, foreign colonists from the outside were brought in to fill the vacancies in population.[17]

Also in the years that followed, the Assyrian importations continued. During the reigns of Esarhaddon and Assurbanipal, for example, additional residents were added to the population in and around Samaria. On one occasion when some of these people were denied an opportunity to help rebuild the temple in Jerusalem, they identified themselves as those who had been brought in by Esarhaddon, while a second group, in writing a letter of complaint to the king of Persia, was referred to as captives dating to the time of *Asnappar*, who most likely was Ashurbanipal.

> Then they came to Zerubbabel, and to the chief of the fathers, and said unto them, Let us build with you: for we seek your God, as ye do; and we do sacrifice unto him since the days of Esarhaddon king of Assur, which brought us up hither.
>
> Then wrote Rehum the chancellor, and Shimshai the scribe, and the rest of their companions; the Dinaites, the Apharsathchites, the Tarpelites, the Apharsites, the Archevites, the Babylonians, the Susanchites, the Dehavites, and the Elamites, and the rest of the nations whom the great and noble Asnappar brought over and set in the cities of Samaria, and the rest that are on this side the river and at such a time.[18]

Following the earlier conquest of Samaria, as recorded

in Assyrian records, the city also allegedly took part in an anti-Assyrian rebellion. There is no scriptural basis for such an event, but the records of Sargon definitely state that during the second year of his reign, he defeated a coalition of states led by the leader of Hamath in Syria, a man named Illubidi. Those participating with him were reportedly Arpad, Simirra, Damascus, and Samaria, as well as possibly a city or place called Hatarikka. In a battle at Qarqar, Sargon subdued the rebels, burned the city, and flayed Illubidi. Moreover, he confiscated two hundred chariots and six hundred cavalry from the enemy forces and added them to his army.[19]

This kind of situation consequently resulted in a number of scholars later advocating two conquests of Samaria instead of one, the event evidently recorded in the Bible and a subsequent one following a rebellion. Also one source says that Sargon did not remove any prisoners at all from the area until about 719 B.C. when he was returning from a campaign in Egypt.[20]

As a consequence of these events and circumstances, therefore, the once-proud Israelite capital experienced more than its share of trauma and difficulty. It is difficult especially to imagine the adverse conditions that must have existed inside the city walls during the many months of siege and conflict. And following these there were the problems of reconstruction and the influx of foreign settlers.

Certainly the situation might have been little better, if not considerably worse, than that of Israelite kinsmen in captivity further to the north. In places such as Haran, Guzana, and Halah, in fact, as well as in various cities of Media, the conditions and standard of living were possibly much more tolerable than those which existed back in Palestine. The benefits of living under a stable and consistent government, even in times of slavery or captivity, have often surpassed those possessed by people in less favorable circumstances who have a greater amount of freedom.

As for the captives in Assyria, their lives continued in the usual way, and at least some of them would one day leave their place of confinement and travel into the north country. Being unaware of what was ahead of them or to which area they were going, they would cross over the narrow passages of the Euphrates River and eventually set their course of direction toward the north. In a very real sense, the polestar would be their guide until such time that they reached a possible *embarkation point*, from which place they would "leave the multitude of the nations and go to a more distant region where mankind had never lived," there to enter a new area and homeland which had been prepared for them.

But in the meantime, those left behind in the original homeland entered a very new phase of existence, joining with incoming colonists from surrounding nations and paying allegiance to the new government and province of Assyria!

The Remnants

Following a rebellion in outlying areas, it was customary for Assyria to implement a systematic procedure in dealing with the problem. This usually included a six-point process of subjugation.

1. Conquest.
2. Partial deportation of population.
3. Rebuilding of a city.
4. Importation of foreign colonists.
5. Organizing a province and appointing a governor.
6. Establishing taxation.

Although the Bible says very little about these aspects, historically they were present. Certainly the Assyrians were interested in regulating and strengthening the different parts of their empire. In restoring stability to a conquered area, they wanted it to be self-sufficient and productive, and even in such things as taxation, it was a matter of regarding people in the outlying provinces basically in the same way as with ordinary citizenry.

The government did not want a large populace of prisoners and dissidents, in other words, but rather groups of people that would work together and make significant contributions to the growth of the empire. In the view of the Assyrians, they, as well as deportees, existed mainly as citizens instead of slaves, although at the same time those taken captive often served as hostages, in a sense, to help keep people in line who were left behind.[21]

Also in regard to the Israelites who remained in northern and central Palestine, along with the people in Transjordan, the Bible has little to say on this subject as well. Yet there are certain instances in which these remnants are clearly mentioned. During the reign of Hezekiah, for example, who was a king in neighboring Judah, some of them were among those invited to a special feast of the passover, an event that took place approximately six years after the fall of Samaria.

> And Hezekiah sent to all Israel and Judah, and wrote letters also to Ephraim and Manasseh, that they should come to the house of the Lord at Jerusalem, to keep the passover unto the Lord God of Israel.
>
> So the posts went with the letters from the king and his princes throughout all Israel and Judah, and according to the commandment of the king, saying, Ye children of Israel, turn again unto the Lord God of Abraham, Isaac, and Israel, and he will return to the remnant of you that are escaped out of the hand of the kings of Assyria.[22]

The reaction of those contacted, however, was not always positive. As the messengers traveled throughout the cities as far north as Asher and Zebulun, they were scorned and rebuked by many of the people, including those in Ephraim and Manasseh. Yet the scripture tells how some did respond, along with certain "strangers that came out of the land of Israel,"[23] and they agreed to make the trip to Jerusalem.

Almost a century later, a similar situation occurred which again included the remnants of the ten tribes residing in Palestine. This was during the time of Josiah, also a king of Judah, and like Hezekiah before him, he initiated religious reforms and held a special passover in Jerusalem.

"For in the eighth year of his reign, while he was yet young, he began to seek after the God of David his father: and in the twelfth year he began to purge Judah and Jerusalem from the high places, and the groves, and the carved images, and the molten images." "And so did he in the cities of Manasseh, and Ephraim, and Simeon, even unto Naphtali, with their mattocks round about."

Then after about six years, Josiah kept the passover in Jerusalem at which "all Judah and Israel" were present. The feast was an elaborate one and surpassed all others that had previously been held. Also during this same time period, there is mention of those who collected money from the various tribes throughout Palestine, including the remnants, for the repair and renovation of the temple.

> And when they came to Hilkiah the high priest, they delivered the money that was brought into the house of God, which the Levites that kept the doors had gathered of the hand of Manasseh and Ephraim, and of all the remnant of Israel, and of all Judah and Benjamin; and they returned to Jerusalem.[24]

Once again, therefore, it is evident that one hundred years after the second invasion and the fall of Samaria, many of those among the ten tribes were still living in the Israelite provinces of the Assyrian Empire. This would continue during the subsequent domination by the Chaldeans of Babylonia who conquered the areas of both Israel and Judah. And then much later, as a historic aftermath, there would be the twenty-five centuries of scattering and dispersing among the nations, all being in connection with another kindred group somewhere pertaining to the north country, those who were also Israelites and who someday would be regarded as the lost tribes of the house of Israel!

Areas of Captivity

When the captives from the ten tribes were deported to the north, they were taken to a region in the upper reaches of the Tigris and Euphrates Rivers and into certain cities of Media farther to the east. The biblical record gives a variety of names to these different areas.

1. Halah
2. Hara
3. Habor
4. the river Gozan
5. cities of the Medes

Although the location of some of the places is undetermined, or at least vague in description, others are more familiar. The place called Hara, for example, also possibly spelled Haran or Harran, might be the same area in upper Mesopotamia where Abraham first settled after leaving Ur of the Chaldees. Located on the Balikh River which flows into the Euphrates, it was a well-known trading center of considerable importance

Another area was Gozan or Guzana, situated approximately fifty miles east of Hara on the headwaters of the Khabur River, also a tributary to the Euphrates. This was a place familiar to archeologists in later times and was referred to as Tell Halaf.

The way the Bible describes what happened at this latter location is that some of the captives were taken to "Habor by the river of Gozan." And yet a more correct reference to the area would be that of a town, city, or province named Gozan or Guzana, situated on the river called Khabur. Using the biblical spelling, therefore, the correct terminology would be *Gozan by the river Habor.*

The place known as Halah is more difficult to identify, but the likely possibility is that it was located northeast of the Assyrian city of Nineveh on the Upper Zab River. Also called Halahhi or Halahhu, it was one of several areas to which both Tiglath-Pileser and Sargon sent prisoners following their invasions.

Finally in the cities of the Medes east of Assyria proper, there were undoubtedly numerous places where evacuees could have been taken. Tiglath-Pileser and Sargon both waged wars in this region, sending prisoners to distant places and also importing others.

The more definitive areas of Assyrian captivity, however, were those closer to the center of the empire, namely Haran, Gozan, and Halah. These were places which are specifically mentioned in various published sources, and although the information given is usually brief and without detail, still it is possible to get from them a general idea of the existence and geographic location of the ten tribes during their deportation and stay in Assyria.

In regard to Haran, it is especially interesting that the former residence of Abraham, as well as that of his brother Nahor and his descendants, should possibly end up being one of the areas of captivity for members of the ten tribes. It was to Haran that Abraham sent one of his servants to find a wife for his son Isaac, and also to the same city that Jacob later went to get away from his brother Esau.

In Jacob's case, he intended to stay only briefly at the time, yet he remained in Haran for many years where he married and had a family. In this place were born eleven of his twelve sons who became heads of the twelve tribes of Israel. Certainly it is ironic that hundreds of years later some of the descendants of these same people might have been brought to the identical area and subjected to Assyrian captivity.

But still an exact identification of this and other such places in the Bible often remains very difficult, and in connection with Haran, it might be that the biblical name of Hara actually refers to some other location, or that it does not mean a city or district at all but rather a range of mountains. One theory has it, for example, that the original text containing this particular name read "hare Madai," translated as *mountains of Media*, and was the same area mentioned in corresponding scriptures as the *cities of the Medes*. The problem arose when the word *madai* was theoretically dropped from the text for some reason, leaving only the word *hare* which was then changed to the proper name Hara.[25]

In the book of 1 Chronicles, it states that some of the Israelites in the first Assyrian invasion were taken captive to Hara but makes no mention of the cities of the Medes. Then in 2 Kings, in connection with the second invasion, it says that prisoners were sent to the cities of the Medes yet says nothing about Hara, the implication being that in these two instances, the name in question might refer to something other than a city, such as Median mountains.

But despite this questionable situation, the area of Haran still remains significant, since it was only fifty miles from Guzana which is more definite as a captivity site. The idea that Abraham lived for a time in Haran and that some of his descendants were later taken to that same general area as Assyrian captives will therefore continue to be a unique concept and matter of interest.

And if Haran itself does turn out to be the place in

question, being in the upper part of Mesopotamia, it would be an ideal location to coincide with the departure of the ten tribes into the north, concerning which an apocryphal description states that "they went in by the narrow passages of the Euphrates River," and "the Most High performed signs for them and stopped the channels of the river until they had passed over."[26]

The same would be true of the region known as Guzana, fifty miles to the east and still very close to the upper part of the Euphrates. It is also this particular city, located on the Habor or Khabur River, that contains additional information, albeit it small and lacking in detail, pertaining to the ten tribes in their captivity area. The city was apparently the capital of the province in which the captives resided and was situated in a part of the country that for centuries had been only pasture land. This was eventually cultivated and turned into a fertile agricultural area that could be of benefit to the Assyrian Empire.

Since agriculture was the economic basis of Assyrian society, it was natural for the government to place many of its deportees in rural areas, especially people who had previously been farmers and shepherds in their own homelands. This is evident in Guzana, as well as in Halah farther east, where captives were given land, vineyards, and orchards, along with necessary animals and machinery, all for the purpose of improving the area and increasing agricultural produce.

At the same time, the imperial revenue was increased through tribute and taxation which, according to one source, consisted not only of silver exacted from deportees but also such things as livestock and agricultural products.[27]

In addition, the idea of taxation itself provides further information pertaining to the tribes in captivity. It was Assyria's policy, for example, to tax captive people in the provinces in basically the same way as ordinary citizens. There was allegedly no distinction between the indigenous population in a conquered territory and incoming deportees. Both groups were considered to be citizens of the empire and therefore subject to governmental requirements.

In this connection, as recorded in some of the Assyrian documents, it is interesting that people in Guzana and a city named Barhalzi to the southwest of nearby Halah were cited on one occasion for being derelict in the payment of their taxes. No mention is made of any punishment, however, which suggests that captives living in the area definitely had a more preferred status than that of slaves or indentured servants.[28]

A distinctive characteristic of Assyrian deportation, in fact, was the idea of a *shared citizenry*. Depending upon the situation, it was more profitable from both a military and economic point of view to have captives who had certain privileges and who felt that they were more than just prisoners. They had to obey rules and pay taxes, as did everyone else, but the benefits they received from the government in other ways helped to make up for it.

Further examples of this, as well as other aspects, can be found among deportees which were located in Halah, the third place of captivity mentioned in the Bible. This area was apparently located about seventy-five miles northeast of Nineveh on or near the Upper Zab River. Also spelled Halahhi or Halahhu, it was an area relatively undefined today, and yet there are scattered references to it in Assyrian documents and correspondence that give significant clues.

One record, for example, states that some of the agricultural fields in Halah belonged to the king and were distributed to temples or high ranking officials. They in turn allotted them to deportees, or in some instances the king would make the assignment himself. In any case, captives ended up occupying and working the land, and the same type of thing evidently existed in Barhalzi immediately to the southwest.[29]

Also there were instances in which captives and their descendants acquired various kinds of real estate, including houses, gardens, and fields. This condition is alluded to in a list of land plots pertaining specifically to the province of Halah where west Semitic names of *Baraki* and *Haannii* are involved. A similar type of name is connected with a vineyard sale in the same province, all of which reflects the Assyrian policy of encouraging captive people to disassociate themselves from their former homeland and establish roots in a new place.[30]

As a final note, and in addition to the political and economic aspects pertaining to Haran, Guzana, and Halah, it is significant that all three of these areas were generally located in an east-west line with one another, extending for approximately two hundred and fifty miles. In contrast, the unidentified places referred to as *the cities of the Medes* were considerably farther to the east, well beyond Assyria proper. As a consequence, there was an important distinction between the two locations, and their separation suggests that there might have been a restricting division among the ten tribes when the time came for at least some of them to leave their places of captivity and travel to the north.

One thing does appear certain, however, and that is that such a departure eventually did occur, possibly around 600 B.C., after which a historic journey began. It was a journey that involved a very specific group of Israelites who traveled into the north country, seeking "a more distant region where mankind had never lived, that there at least they might keep their statutes which they had not kept in their own land."[31] In doing so, they followed a way marked by Deity itself to a place of remoteness and seclusion, the location of which is unknown, and there at an undetermined point in time, they mysteriously passed from among the nations and completely disappeared!

Conditions and Circumstances

It is important to remember that only part of the ten tribes were taken into captivity. This was in line with Assyrian deportation policy, which was that approximately one half of a population would be removed and the other half left to be the substructure for incoming colonists.[32]

One source has it that most of the people were actually left behind, and another that only about one out of twenty was taken from the northern kingdom.[33] And whereas these statements generally represent extreme viewpoints, they do emphasize the idea that total deportation, or very close to it as is sometimes suggested in the Bible, is probably inaccurate and untrue.

A significant thing to consider is the claims made by Tiglath-Pileser III and Sargon II as to how many people they actually took captive. During his invasion of Transjordan and northern Palestine, for example, the first king reportedly took only 13,520 prisoners, and the second, following the conquest of Samaria, a total of 27,280.[34] Comparing these figures with the population that must have existed in the Kingdom of Israel at the time, it is very possible that the number of captives deported to Assyria might have been considerably less than what normally might be expected.

This in turn suggests that those who did go into captivity were a select and representative group. And for whatever reason, and assuming that the purposes of Deity were involved, at least some of these people would later be chosen to represent all of the ten tribes in a bold new adventure that would take them to a different part of the earth. Serving as an experimental group, as it were, they would be tried and tested under a very different set of circumstances, one that would exclusively set them apart down through the ages and eventually give them the name of *the lost tribes of Israel*, following which the intention was that someday they would rejoin normal society.

Yet in relation to the Assyrian invasions and conquests, this latter event was still far in the future. Twenty-five centuries of world history and temporal existence were yet to take place as a lone and solitary people continued to fulfill a prophetic destiny. And previous to all of this, as a necessary and dramatic prelude, were the long years of Israelite captivity!

Indeed, for the deportees who found themselves in Hara, Guzana, and Halah, as well as in the distant cities of the Medes, this time period was definitely a historic era, one that involved a new setting and culture and at least four new generations. It was also a time which saw the nation of Assyria rise to its greatest height as a Middle Eastern power and then within a hundred years begin an inevitable decline.

During the reigns of Tiglath-Pileser and Sargon, however, Assyria continued to show few signs of weakening. To the contrary, the nation became increasingly stronger, with each military victory being a reminder that the Assyrian objective without question was that of ruling the world. This was especially exemplified by Sargon who, in connection with his invasions, built a brand new city and capital named Dur-Sharrukin, also known as Sargonsburg, to which undertaking he brought builders and craftsmen from all over the empire, including qualified people among captives and deportees.

When the capital city of Samaria was captured, for example, in the year 721 B.C., some of the prisoners were immediately conscripted into the Assyrian army while others were taken to "the midst of Assyria." The situation of the latter group suggests that those more adapted to agriculture were removed to rural areas while laborers and craftsmen might have been sent to the inner cities, especially to the site of the new city of Dur-Sharrukin. It is most likely that some of those among the ten tribes became involved in such projects.

Again it was not Assyria's intent to make slaves of its conquered people. Rather the plan was to utilize the ability and capacity of prisoners to the advantage of the empire and to position them geographically according to their trades and craft. People taken to large cities such as Nineveh, Ashur, and Calah, in other words, were possibly engaged in the building of temples and palaces, while those in Guzana and Halah would more likely be involved in agriculture and food production.

And yet there were instances where a particular locality might have been characterized by both conditions. This was true on one occasion when a group of men and their sons, twenty-five in number and all of them craftsmen, were brought to Guzana. At another time, persons from Rasappa and Arzuhina, and possibly Guzana again, were apparently sent to Dur-Sharrukin to help build Sargon's city.[35]

In connection with these situations, it is interesting that one of the Assyrian inscriptions pertaining to "the city of Gozan," or Guzana, refers to an individual named *Halbishu the Samarian*. His true identity is not given, although obviously he was someone who might been deported from Samaria. Another inscription, this one relating to the province of Halah, mentions a certain *Ahiqam*, a person possessing a Hebrew name and possibly also an Israelite deportee.[36]

Such instances are brief and scattered, of course, but they do allude to the presence of people among the ten tribes and continue to give evidence that they were in this general area.

Still a more substantial piece of information is found on a stone prism discovered at Calah, also known as Nimrud. It contains Sargon's personal account and description of what happened during the conquest of Samaria and makes particular mention of prisoners taken into the military.

"The man of Samaria and a king who was hostile to me," he said, "had joined together to refuse homage and tribute to me, and came out to fight with me. By the help of the great gods, my lords, I overthrew them: I captured from them 27,280 persons with their chariots, their gods in whom they trusted, and took as my royal share of the booty two hundred chariots. I gave orders that the rest should be settled in the midst of Assyria."[37]

Reference to two hundred chariots would also undoubtedly include the two hundred men who drove them, and as it turned out, these eventually became a significant addition to Sargon's army. From the beginning they were organized into a unit and appear to have become a well-known cohort in the Assyrian cavalry. They were under the control of an officer named *Nebubeluukin,* and under him were fifteen military commanders, most whom allegedly had west Semitic names.

Ibbadalaa	Iaugaa	Papidri
Enbad	Pap	Dalapap
Papiu	Gabbie	Atamru
Abdimilku	Naarmenaa	Samaa
Bahie	Papidri	Pauginin

The names of these commanders were listed in a roll call in connection with one of Sargon's campaigns against the Babylonians in 710–708 B.C., some twelve years after the fall of Samaria. The list is the only one among others stating a specific place of origin for personnel, which suggests that this particular unit might have had a significant reputation.[38] Soldiers from the northern kingdom in Palestine, in fact, were well-known for their chariot driving, as well as the ability to use Nubian horses.[39] But whatever the group's status, its existence in the Assyrian army at this time gives valuable information and presents another interesting sidelight to the account of Israelite captivity!

Attitude toward Prisoners

Whenever the subject of Assyria is encountered in world history, one of the first things that comes to mind is the military, especially methods of warfare and the ruthlessness of commanders and personnel. This one country, possibly above all others, was known for its violence and inhumane treatment of conquered people.

Assyrian soldiers were reputed to have an inborn ferocity which made them a threat and terror to surrounding nations. There are many stories of cruelty and torture, such as prisoners being skinned alive and impaled upon stakes while their chief men and rulers marched with the heads of former princes hung around their necks.

Yet with all of the references to barbarism and atrocity, there is also the other side to Assyrian militarism. First of all, it might be that Assyria was not so different from other nations of that time period in the way they conducted their warfare. The thing that especially characterized them and set them apart was the way they publicized it. The king and his military commanders made it a point of boasting about their cruelty, whereas in actuality they were maybe no more guilty of it sometimes than others around them. It was their main intent to discourage rebellion, and an important way of accomplishing this was by way of propaganda and intimidation.[40]

In the case of the Israelites, they were warned ahead of time about the danger of Assyria, yet in the conquest of Transjordan and northern Palestine, as well as Samaria, the biblical record says nothing about cruelty or fatalities, only that people were taken captive. Violence was undoubtedly present, particularly in regard to rebellious rulers, but concerning prisoners in general, the idea of brutality and inhumane treatment mentioned in secular sources has possibly been overemphasized.

Another positive aspect of the Assyrian military was the efficient and systematic way in which they conducted deportations. In general, prisoners were not abused but were protected and well taken care of so they would arrive at their places of captivity in good condition. Deportees were a valuable commodity, as it were, and it was important for them to stay healthy in order to be of maximum benefit to the king and his government.

In addition, it was often Assyrian policy to deport people by families. In this way they discouraged prisoners from trying to escape and also improved the prospects of them being able to settle down and establish roots in a new place. And whereas a family-type system of deportation might at first appear incongruous with warlike Assyria, it was the idea once again of doing things politically, as well as militarily and economically, and in this way convert dissatisfied captives into productive citizens of the empire.[41]

Not only was there deportation by families, but also sometimes by communities. In preserving the communal organization of captives, the Assyrians hoped to keep them more contained in their new areas and give them the feeling that they were still dwelling among their own people. They were free to retain ancestral customs and traditions and also conduct their own community affairs as long as it did not conflict with imperial interests.

Again this might appear inconsistent in regard to a nation like Assyria that was so feared and hated throughout the Middle East. Yet it seems to have been a common policy. It was not that the Assyrian king was a humanitarian, but rather a wise administrator and politician. He wanted to make sure that captives were an asset to the government and not a liability.

As a consequence, while people were en route to a destination they were monitored closely by appointed officials who were responsible to see that there was no abuse or exploitation. Keeping prisoners supplied with food and provisions was especially important, as was their personal safety, during what was usually a long journey. Governors of the different territories through which they traveled were instructed to look after them and help meet their needs.[42]

In connection with all of these factors, therefore, it seems likely that those among the ten tribes who were taken captive to Assyria made a successful transfer from Transjordan and Palestine to their new homes in the north. For the ones who stopped in Guzana, and possibly Haran, this journey was relatively short, while the trip to Halah and surrounding areas undoubtedly took considerably longer.

And for those who for whatever reason went farther east to the more distant cities of the Medes, there could have been an extremely long travel time, one estimate being several years, in order to reach a vague and obscure destination. This latter group, in fact, whose designated area is associated with the controversial name of Hara, continues to be an enigma and question mark in the account of the lost tribes of Israel, yet at the same time a very significant part of a much larger unsolved mystery!

The Media Problem

Somewhere in Media, south of Lake Urmia and in the vicinity of the Zagros Mountains, part of the ten tribes finally arrived at their distant place of captivity. Separated from the Israelites who were located several hundred miles to the west, they now found themselves in an unfamiliar and relatively isolated area.

Their present location was in the region known today as western Iran and was on the eastern edge of the Assyrian Empire. Divided politically into a large number of city states and villages, it was the site of numerous invasions by both Tiglath-Pileser III and Sargon II.

In the extensive mountain region connecting Assyria proper and the land of Media, for example, Tiglath-Pileser ravaged a wide area of territory, deporting an alleged total of sixty-five thousand of its inhabitants and eventually replacing them with people from other countries. This type of subjugation also continued during the reign of Sargon, one instance being the fortified city of Harhar, which was on the road leading from Assyria and very close to the Median border.

In 716 B.C., five years after the conquest of Samaria, Sargon conquered this area, again removing captives and prisoners and bringing in foreign colonists. He rebuilt the city of Harhar and called it Kar-Sharrukin.

In connection with these invasions, it is recorded that the rulers in twenty-eight adjoining Median city states ended up paying tribute to Sargon, increasing the empire's sphere of influence more than ever before. The same was true two years later prior to a campaign against Urartu when more kings in Media paid tribute.

Then again during the following year of 713 B.C., as Assyria was quelling a rebellion in Ellipi, no less than forty-five Median heads of state reportedly declared their allegiance to the Assyrian government. This was likely in geographical areas where deportations and importations were taking place, which consequently made them potential locations pertaining to the ten tribes. Any of the settlements in this region, in fact, might be considered as "cities of the Medes."[43]

All of this alludes once more to a condition of remoteness and isolation and to the question of why some of the Israelite captives were settled in such outlying areas while others ended up closer to the center of the empire. It is the question of what purpose it served, if any, as far as the Israelites were concerned, to have this kind of separation, and also how many people were involved.

Obviously there could be different reasons for what happened, but certainly one of them, especially from the vantage point of Assyria, pertained to the two-way system of deportation. This means that whenever prisoners were evacuated from cities in Media or elsewhere, it was necessary to bring in comparable numbers from the outside to take their place. In addition, there was always the need for incoming people who could contribute to internal stability as well as help defend vulnerable borders of the empire.

Possibly the main reason, however, in regard to the Israelites themselves, is that there was a religious purpose involved. In other words, the Israelite captivity was not just one of many deportations at that time, but rather a very specific one, a part of which would one day break away from the others and embark upon an eventful journey further into the north country. And when this event finally occurred, it might be that captives in the east, because of their remoteness, would be less apt to be included than those in the west.

Yet again this presents a continuing problem, one which involves the correct identification of a place or city in the western part of the empire and also a scriptural interpretation. Were some of the Israelite captives placed in Haran in northwestern Mesopotamia, for example, or does *Hara* in the Bible refer instead to certain mountainous areas in Media? And if the latter is true, how far into Media were people taken? Was it east of the Zagros Mountains or more toward the west?

The possibility always remains that the name *Hara*, which in Hebrew means "mountain, hill country, or highland," does not refer to the place called Haran but rather to *Median mountains* or *cities*. This is suggested partially by the fact that the word in question occurs in 1 Chronicles 5:26 in the Bible but not elsewhere, including the same scripture in the Septuagint, the Greek translation of the Old Testament.

"And the God of Israel stirred up the spirit of Pul king of Assyria," the Bible states, " and the spirit of Tilgath-pilneser king of Assyria, and he carried them away, even the Reubenites, and the Gadites, and the half tribe of Manasseh, and brought them unto Halah, and Habor, and Hara, and to the river Gozan, unto this day."

Further evidence is found in 2 Kings 17:6 where the names of Halah, Habor, and Gozan are listed as captivity sites, along with cities of the Medes, but no mention is made of Hara. Again the same is true in the Septuagint except that the wording in this second scripture says *mountains* of the Medes instead of *cities*.

"In the ninth year of Hoshea," according to the Bible, "the king of Assyria took Samaria, and carried Israel away into Assyria, and placed them in Halah and in Habor by the river of Gozan, and in the cities of the Medes."

Once more the theory is that the original manuscript of 1 Chronicles listed the places of captivity as they now appear in the Septuagint and 2 Kings, including reference to Median mountains or cities (*hare Madai* or *are Madai*). But at a later time, the word Madai disappeared from the text for some reason, leaving only the word *Hare* or *Are* which in turn was changed to the proper name of Hara.

There are other interpretations for Hara, such as a town in northern Mesopotamia called *Ara*, as well as *Aria* which is another name for Media, and less likely also the city of *Harhar*. But Haran on the Balikh River, with its significant background in Old Testament history, is still a definite possibility.

Moreover, in regard to this last theory, there are at least four examples of supporting evidence. (1) In the two accounts pertaining to the first Assyrian invasion, namely that of Transjordan in 1 Chronicles as well as northern Palestine in 2 Kings, no mention is made of any people being deported specifically to Media. Also the fact that no places of captivity are mentioned at all in the second account suggests that they were probably the same as that of the first, considering that the two Israelite areas were so close together. In other words, in the initial invasion it was a matter of removing people to the three locations of Haran, Guzana, and Halah, all on a line with one another and extending for about two hundred and fifty miles.

(2) It is inconsistent to exclude Haran as a captivity site and at the same time include nearby Guzana and Halah. All three cities existed together as a unit in a logical geographical area, a situation that is partially alluded to in an incident during the reign of Hezekiah, a king of Judah.

The time period was about 700 B.C., and the Assyrians had again invaded Palestine under Sennacherib, conquering all of the Judean cities except Jerusalem. On two different occasions the king sent messengers to Hezekiah, reminding him and his people of Assyria's previous conquests and power and encouraging them to surrender. Among the messengers was a man named Rabshekeh, who could speak to the people in their own language and who some have conjectured was a former Israelite deportee.

"Behold, thou hast heard what the kings of Assyria have done to all lands," a messenger said, "by destroying them utterly: and shalt thou be delivered? Have the gods of the nations delivered them which my fathers have destroyed; as Gozan, and Haran, and Rezeph, and the children of Eden which were in Thelasar?"[44]

Both Haran and Gozan, or Guzana, therefore, were not only well-known places of conquest but most likely captivity sites as well.

(3) Two invasions of the kingdom of Israel by Assyria, one in approximately 732 B.C. and the other in 724 B.C., possibly included the same places of captivity except for the cities or mountains of Media. The latter location could have pertained only to those people taken in the *second* invasion at the time of the conquest of Samaria, which would be a logical circumstance since Media was so far removed to the east.

(4) The different theories of how the name Hara originated in the Bible are interesting, but as one source has put it, they involve "a complicated series of technical problems."[45] In view of this it might be that things have been made much more complicated than necessary. Consequently, regardless of the number of arguments against the case for Haran as a captivity site, there are at the same time a considerable number that are for it.

The main thing is that there were two separate areas in the Assyrian Empire where Israelites from the ten tribes were taken, one in the west and the other in the east, and whether or not the city of Haran was included in the former is probably not that important. What is significant is that the tribes were definitely separated, even within the western region of Halah and Guzana, and when the time came for some of them to move, their different conditions and geographic locations might or might not have been a factor.

It is possible, in fact, that only a certain percentage among the tribes actually made the journey into the north country. Certainly an unusual combination of circumstances was involved at this point in history, one that set a particular group of people apart from all others and marked them for a specific purpose and destiny. But when the time did come for them to begin their journey, they were ready, and although the prospects ahead were uncertain, they left their places of captivity with resolution and headed toward the north!

The City of Dur-Sharrukin

One of the reasons that the ten tribes made their move when they did might well have been because Assyria was in the process of being replaced by Chaldea as the dominant power in the Middle East. Or it could have been at an earlier time period. The movement of a sizeable group of people, however, leaving a populated area and traveling to the north, would suggest that political conditions had changed and that such an occurrence was now more of a possibility.

But if the migration did take place while the Assyrians were still in power, it seems likely that it would have been soon after the reigns of Sennacherib, Esarhaddon, and Ashurbanipal, the last of the well-known kings. During the twenty years that followed, while things were rapidly deteriorating, a departure under cover might have been much less monitored.

Tiglath-Pileser III	744–727
Shalmaneser V	726–722
Sargon II	721–705
Sennacherib	704–681
Esarhaddon	680–669
Assurbanipal	668–627
Final Period of Rulers	626–606

The six kings of Assyria beginning with Tiglath-Pileser III were undoubtedly the most outstanding of the empire and can be regarded distinctively as a separate group or dynasty. Yet the three that came at the last were noticeably different from those at the first, which might partly explain why the tribes left when they did.

The practice of a *shared citizenry*, for example, among indigenous populations and deportees, appears especially to have been a distinguishing characteristic of the first group. Time after time, Tiglath-Pileser and Sargon both stated that in relocating conquered people they counted them as regular subjects of Assyria, bonafide citizens of the empire and not as serfs or slaves.

Such a policy apparently changed, however, during the administration of the next three kings. For whatever reasons, they no longer referred to a shared citizenship.[46] This did not necessarily mean a radical change for all captives, but as the empire grew, there was more of a demand for manpower in connection with road construction, irrigation, the building of palaces and temples, and reconstruction of towns and cities. An increasing number of the subject population was consequently needed for work projects, as well as for service in the military. It might be that increased pressure on the Israelites, therefore, sometime after the reign of Sargon, was one of the reasons why at least some of them eventually decided to travel toward the north.

And yet the need for manpower itself was nothing new and had always been a significant factor. This was particularly true in 717 B.C. when Sargon commenced his new city and capital at Dur-Sharrukin northeast of Nineveh. The enterprise was a huge undertaking, requiring a virtual army of engineers, workmen, and craftsmen and without question included deportees, some of whom were Israelites. Conquered people from all over the empire were involved in the ten-year project.

Since the deportation of captives was often a selective process, where political figures, craftsmen, and those in the upper classes were taken while others were left behind, it is logical that some of those deported, especially from Samaria, ended up in the construction area at Dur-Sharrukin. People in Guzana and Halah were also in relatively close proximity to the building site and could easily have been conscripted into the work force, either at the time of their deportation or soon after.

On one occasion, in fact, the king wrote to one of his supervisors and told him to provide "all the Samaritans" under his jurisdiction with work in the new city. In response, the latter sent a message to certain *sheiks*, as he called them, instructing them to gather together their carpenters and potters. "Let them come," he said, "and direct the deportees who are in Dur-Sharrukin."

In addition, native citizens in the empire under various work obligations also participated in the project, although it appears mostly to have been captives from the outside. The king in his royal inscriptions states outright that he built Dur-Sharrukin with the labor of foreign people.[47] As a later consequence, deportees who had been involved in the city's construction apparently remained there as a large percentage of its population, being ordered to learn the Assyrian language and show reverence to gods and king.

As for the city itself, it was an extraordinary achievement, not just because of its size and architecture, but because of the phenomenal speed of construction. It was slightly more than ten years between the time that the foundations were laid and the concluding ceremonies held in 707–706 B.C. Indeed Sargon was intent on expediting and intensifying all phases of activity, giving full priority to this particular project. And when it was finished, not completely but enough for dedication and inauguration, he followed it with the customary sacrificing and feasting.

In celebration of the large religious complex situated next to the palace, the king extended invitations to all of Assyria's deities, asking them to come to the various temples and shrines where he could make appropriate sacrifices to them. These included "Assur, the father of the gods, the great lord, and all the great gods" who dwelt in Assyria. He then staged a royal banquet to which were invited the important nobles, rulers, and princes of the empire. And finally in 706 B.C., the impressive palace and city were formerly inaugurated.

It was a grand occasion, and Sargon anticipated many years in his new capital. In his own words, he said that he looked forward to growing old there. Yet it was all in vain, for only a few months later he fell in battle, and his body was never retrieved for burial. His son Sennacherib then took over as the new Assyrian ruler.[48]

Undoubtedly all of this provided a significant and impressive backdrop for those of the ten tribes who happened to be residing in Dur-Sharrukin. Such would apply also to those in nearby Halah and Guzana. At the same time, it was a reminder that Israelite captivity was not necessarily a matter of people being in imprisonment or slavery, but rather in more ordinary situations where they continued as families and enjoyed at least a reasonable amount of freedom and normal activity.

Yet in addition, especially for the Israelites living in Dur-Sharrukin, and possibly those also in nearby Nineveh, it must have been a time of worry and uncertainty, not knowing how things would be for them now as a new king took over and assumed his rightful place in the empire!

Tobit in Nineveh

According to the book of Tobias in the Apocrypha, there were also Israelite captives living in Nineveh, people who had been conquered by Sargon in northern Palestine.[49] And although the Bible says nothing about captives taken to this area, the apocryphal account tells how Tobit of the tribe of Naphtali was deported there with his family, later gaining favor with the king, who is referred to as Enemessar, and being designated as *purveyor* or supplier of food and provisions.

As the story goes, Tobit made it a practice, along with his other duties, of looking after his brethren, giving them alms and providing food and clothing where needed. He also secretly buried any of his people whom he found dead or slain about the city of Ninevah. Especially during the following reign of Sennacherib, who in his wrath slew many Israelites upon returning from an invasion of the kingdom of Judah, Tobit was kept busy burying dead bodies.

But the day came when someone complained to the king about what was happening, and Tobit temporarily had to leave the city and flee for his life. All of his property was taken from him, and he was left alone with only his wife and a son named Tobias.

A short time later, however, the political situation changed. Sennacherib was assassinated, and his son Sarchedonus, or Esarhaddon, became king. He appointed a man named Achiacherus to be over all of his father's accounts, as well as his own personal affairs, and by a fortunate circumstance, the latter turned out to be Tobit's nephew who was able to arrange for his uncle to come out of hiding and return to Nineveh.

Much like Joseph of Egypt, Achiacherus was the king's cupbearer and keeper of the signet, a steward and overseer of the royal accounts. The scripture in the Apocrypha states that Esarhaddon actually "appointed him next unto him."[50]

Certainly because of his association with Achiacherus, things went well for Tobit, and he was able to move freely about the empire. Earlier he had traveled eastward to the city of Rages in Media where he placed ten talents of silver in the trust of a man named Gabael, the brother of Gabrias. Both were evidently Israelites spending time in Assyrian captivity.

And then at a later date, Tobit's son Tobias also went to Media, to the capital city of Ecbatana where he met an Israelite girl whom he eventually married. The girl's name was Sara, the daughter of Raguel who was Tobit's cousin.

An interesting thing about these journeys, of course, the first one by Tobit and the second by his son, is the interaction which took place between captives living in the central part of Assyria and those farther east in the two Median cities. It obviously suggests that despite considerable distances involved, communication between these two Israelite groups did occur, and also that some of those in the more eastern areas of the empire might very possibly have been involved in a later migration of the ten tribes.

Yet whatever it was that happened, Tobit eventually gave a dire warning of what was in the future as far as Nineveh was concerned. On his death bed, he talked about the prophecies of Jonah and advised his son and family to flee to the cities in the east. The city of Nineveh would definitely be overthrown, he told them, and "for a time peace shall rather be in Media."[51]

And Tobias did as his father said, taking his wife and children and returning to Ecbatana, in which place he was living on the day that he heard Nineveh had been destroyed.

The book of Tobit, therefore, despite its questionable authenticity as part of the Apocrypha, and also certain chronological problems, provides important information pertaining to the Israelite tribes in captivity. In addition, it is a recall of certain conditions existing back in Palestine. One thing of significance, for example, is that although the Bible tells how Tiglath-Pileser III deported captives from Transjordan and northern Palestine, it says nothing about his successor Sargon II ever taking any people from those same areas. Yet in the apocryphal account, Tobit definitely says that it was the latter king who deported him and his people from the tribe of Naphtali, "out of Thisbe, which is at the right hand of that city, which is called properly Nephthali in Galilee above Aser."[52]

When people were exiled from their homeland, located in the northern section of Palestine and anywhere between thirty and sixty miles north of Samaria, they were apparently not always taken to the usual places of Haran, Guzana, and Halah but sometimes directly to the city of Nineveh. Again this provides new information, since there is no mention of the latter in the Bible as a captivity site. The city was relatively close to Halah in the northeast, however, and between these two areas there could have easily been interaction and communication. In fact, it has been said that one of Nineveh's gates was named "the gate of the land of Halahhi."[53]

Another important circumstance mentioned in the book of Tobias is that the ten tribes in general, prior to captivity, had apostatized from the worship of Jehovah and instead were sacrificing to the heifer Baal. The tribe of Naphtali in particular was included. A notable exception was Tobit, however, who earlier had traveled to Jerusalem on feast days and revered the temple that was located there.

But possibly the most significant information pertaining to the situation in Palestine is the fact that Tobit makes no mention of the Assyrian conquest of Samaria. There is nothing in his record pertaining to the downfall of the northern Israelite capital and kingdom.

Traditionally it has been a matter of Sargon exiling the ten tribes from the capital city, with no reference to Israelites who had been taken from Transjordan and the north of Palestine. And this by itself is not surprising, since in one sense Samaria was symbolic of all the kingdom of Israel just as the name of Ephraim was used in much the same way.

Yet certainly Tobit residing in Nineveh, being situated so close to Haran and Guzana, and particularly to Halah, would not only have known of Samaria's fate but would have mentioned it. But he did not, and that remains one of the interesting things about the Israelite story.

It is a small thing, in a way, but if nothing else, it again points to the idea that the phenomenon of the *lost tribes of Israel* contains many unanswered questions and is probably much more unique and complex than previously believed. Many factors are undoubtedly involved that are not mentioned in Assyrian records, the Apocrypha, or the Bible. Circumstances pertaining to the tribes' departure to the north especially remain in question. The people who ultimately made up that particular group, in other words, might have assembled from places all over the empire, scattered populations coming in to a central place in Assyria in order to decide on a final course of action and to devise a plan.

And if that is the way things actually happened, it very dramatically set the stage for one of the most extraordinary occurrences in biblical history, one that very few people know about today but one nevertheless that in some way and at some undetermined time and place actually did occur!

Departure to the North

Information about the departure of the ten tribes to the north country is almost nonexistent. If it were not for the Apocrypha, the noncanonical scriptures of the Old Testament, there would be very little scriptural evidence that such an event ever took place.

But in the book of 2 Esdras, sometimes known as 2 Ezra, one brief statement has been enough to attract people's attention, so much so that many now believe that some of the Israelites in captivity eventually left their places in Assyria and became the so-called *lost tribes of Israel.* In little more than a hundred words, the account tells how a certain group departed from their homes in and around Mesopotamia and traveled to an unknown region called Arzareth.

> But they formed this plan for themselves, that they would leave the multitude of the nations and go to a more distant region, where mankind had never lived, that there at least they might keep their statues which they had not kept in their own land.
>
> And they went in by the narrow passages of the Euphrates River. For at that time the Most High performed signs for them and stopped the channels of the river until they had passed over. Through that region there was a long way to go, a journey of a year and a half; and that country is called Arzareth.[54]

It is significant that such a small passage of scripture could generate all that has been said about the departure of the lost tribes. And yet certainly this is not without precedent. There are any number of instances in the Bible where an important event or principle is documented by only a brief reference.

The statement in Genesis 10:25 is one example, where mention is made of the *division of the earth* during the days of Peleg. Also there is reference to the preexistence of the House of Israel in Deuteronomy 32:8 as well as to an event in Joshua 10:13 where the sun and moon stood still. Such examples are unique and might well imply that scriptures sometimes are purposely veiled in secrecy so that the content involved will remain a matter of nondisclosure.

In any case, the apocryphal account in 2 Esdras is an extremely important statement, and despite its questionable authenticity, it remains the main basis for the idea that the ten tribes disappeared into the north country. Indeed the intent of this group, according to the scripture, was to find a completely unexplored and isolated area where they could begin anew and form a new civilization. And although Assyria and surrounding areas might be regarded as valid *places in the north*, often referred to in the Bible, still a location much further beyond is implied in regard to the lost tribes.

The journey of a year and a half through an unknown region could have taken the people deep into present-day Russia or Scandinavia. That length of time would have allowed them to go to any number of places. Also in relation to the conditions mentioned in the Apocrypha, such as when "the Most High performed signs for the people and stopped the channels of the river," the implication is that more supernatural occurrences lay ahead, those which would ensure not only that the Israelite refugees would reach their destination but would there find complete privacy and seclusion.

Again this establishes the migrating tribes as a very unusual people. They were not the ten tribes per se, in other words, but rather a very select and exclusive group. Very possibly these were people who had been screened and separated along the way and were finally chosen for a specific goal or purpose. For whatever reason, their existence was to be different from all others and their eventual destiny extraordinary and unique.

These were those whose descendants would someday be part of the promised gathering of Israel, yet at the same time also distinctively separate from it. At some future date, at least a portion of their posterity would come out of isolation and seclusion and be restored to the mainstream of society. And on that occasion, after the House of Israel had been scattered and sifted among the nations, a remarkable reunion would take place and Israelites once again would begin to be one people.

Yet in the meantime, while still in Assyrian captivity, thousands were spending their existence in Hara, Guzana, and Halah, as well as possibly in Nineveh and also the cities of the Medes. Enveloped in a new environment, they pursued a variety of occupations including farming, crafts, construction work, and the military, along with common labor. In addition, some were apparently involved in public administration, acting as supervisors of one kind or another and serving as civic officials.

There were probably also those who became so accustomed to their new living place and way of life that they later chose not to leave. Especially with each succeeding generation, people would develop new concepts, as well as new interests and values. But the time eventually arrived, possibly before or shortly after 606 B.C. when the Assyrian Empire came to an end, or even sometime during the following occupation of Mesopotamia by the Chaldeans of Babylonia, when at least some of the people apparently left their homes and traveled to the upper reaches of the Euphrates River, from which place they soon changed their direction and finally began a historic northern journey!

In a Northern Country

In regard to the extraordinary phenomenon of the ten tribes, or at least that part of them which is said to be lost, it is difficult to visualize their true status and to know actually who they are. For centuries their identity has been a question mark and an enigma. Yet one thing is certain, and that is that any reference to the *lost tribes of Israel* needs to be much more definitive than just the ten tribes in general.

The specific people involved, in other words, represent an exclusive group that apparently was set apart in the beginning for a specific goal or mission. At several points along the way, there appears to have been a screening process designed to provide a final segment of Israelite population that would be suitable for some divine purpose.

From the time that the House of Israel was divided into two kingdoms down to the Assyrian conquests and deportations by Tiglath-Pileser, Shalmaneser, and Sargon, as well as possibly by other kings that followed, people were segregated and resettled until the right combination finally occurred. Consequently, it was not just an incidental group that migrated into the north country but a very select union of people.

And yet there is also the question of where the tribes went after traveling northward for a year and a half and reaching a preliminary destination. After traversing the unknown country known as Arzareth, as recorded in the Apocrypha, what was it that happened then?

Some would say that they settled in a northern region and became the nucleus or substructure of a future population. Their destiny, in doing so, was to multiply and diffuse among the nations. Others subscribe to a more imaginative and unorthodox view such as people going into some kind of subterranean area or supernaturally transferring to another sphere or planet. There are really not that many options as to what could have happened to the ten tribes.

But if a plausible option or solution does exist, one that at least partially explains the tribes' mysterious disappearance, it might be that it is found only in two small verses of modern scripture. It could be that the main indication or clue concerning the disappearance of this group of people ironically lies in the prophetic description of their future reappearance and return.

In the book entitled *The Doctrine and Covenants*, for example, which contains a record of any number of miraculous occurrences as well as the alleged revelations of Joseph Smith, the Mormon prophet, the following is recorded in section 133, verses 26 and 27.

> And they who are in the north countries shall come in remembrance before the Lord; and their prophets shall hear his voice and shall no longer stay themselves; and they shall smite the rocks, and the ice shall flow down at their presence. And an highway shall be cast up in the midst of the great deep.

In very few places in recorded scripture is there anything that surpasses the language and content of these two verses. Even for anyone who is well acquainted with the history and background of the twelve tribes of Israel, the information given is almost beyond belief. Not only does it make a prediction as to how the lost tribes will come back in the future, but it also issues an important statement in regard to their mysterious disappearance more than twenty-five hundred years ago.

The fact that rock, ice, and water will play an important part in the tribes' return is definitely a strong implication that the same kind of factors might have been present at the time of their disappearance. This in turn suggests a geographical location in an extremely northern area, one which adjoins a large body of water.

On the other hand, it is claimed by others that the tribes did not travel extensively into the north but settled in a more favorable region where they could keep livestock and raise crops. Here they would be in a more likely position to disperse in different directions and mingle with surrounding nations. Yet in visualizing the time when the tribes return, and considering the unusual circumstances of their predicted reappearance, it is difficult to reconcile any such area with crumbling rock and falling ice.

A more accurate explanation might be that the migrating group did not actually remain in a northern place but merely used it as a *point of embarkation,* as it were, to a still more distant location. In view of this, the rock and ice occurrence described in the Doctrine and Covenants could well imply some kind of *entrance way* for the ten tribes that was comparable to what has been predicted in connection with their *place of exit* in the future!

In regard to the latter, there is no reason to doubt a literal interpretation of the scripture which says that prophets in charge of the returning tribes will actually smite the rocks. Just as Moses of old smote a rock and caused water to flow, so these modern leaders, according to some unknown phenomena, will cause rocks to fall, possibly creating some kind of breach or opening.

There is also the matter of ice flowing down in front of them, suggesting not only a northern location once again but another supernatural occurrence instigated by the Lord through his prophets. The same would be true with the miraculous *highway* that "shall be cast up in the midst of the great deep."

Surely enough cannot be said about these extraordinary events. The different circumstances involved are again almost beyond comprehension. But when they do finally occur, they will not only confirm the words of the scripture but will signal the conclusion of one of the most significant and daring episodes in ancient and modern history.

And although some maintain that the scripture pertaining to rock, ice, and water can still be explained in realistic or symbolic ways, the language expressed is nevertheless sufficiently clear. A religious occurrence of great magnitude is yet to take place. In close proximity to the Battle of Armageddon and the Second Coming of Jesus Christ, it will be an event concluding a dramatic era and dispensation, at the same time revealing the true identity of the lost tribes of Israel and showing what their true reason and purpose have been all down through the ages of time!

A Remarkable Scripture

It is often characteristic of scripture that in a very few words a tremendous truth can be established. Capsulized into a single sentence or paragraph, a highly important thought or idea can be expressed. The Proverbs and the Book of Psalms in the Bible are good examples, and in many other places in literature it is often a very brief statement of something that proves to be the most significant.

Such is the nature of the two small verses in the 133rd section of the Doctrine and Covenants. In slightly more than fifty words this scripture provides extremely valuable information. Each clause and sentence contains a valuable clue as to where the ten tribes might presently be located and in what manner in the future they will return. And even though the material is very brief, it is enough to give considerable preference to one concept over another.

The most prevalent view pertaining to the tribes in general is that they are currently dispersed among the different people of the world. After two and a half millennia and a hundred generations, the descendants of Israelites who used to live in Transjordan and northern and central Palestine are now residing in more than two hundred different countries. Like their kindred in the kingdom of Judah, the former Kingdom of Israel has been scattered in all directions and is thoroughly sifted among the nations, "like as corn is sifted in a sieve."

And again these are definitely true statements, insofar that they do *not* include that portion of the ten tribes who have traditionally been regarded as *lost*. In regard to the lost tribes specifically, in other words, the single scripture in the Doctrine and Covenants is enough to suggest a contrasting idea and a very different concept and viewpoint.

An important factor, for example, in addition to the phenomenon of rock, ice, and water, is that the tribes will be led by *prophets* who have the ability to smite the earth and cause rocks to fall. This in itself gives an entirely new meaning to the predicted return of the tribes. Certainly it suggests that the people will not only be involved in some kind of religious movement but will be coming from a very extraordinary place.

It further implies that they are exiting from a type of environment or geographical area which has provided centuries of isolation apart from regular society. This does not mean just a social or cultural isolation but a very material one that requires a physical removal of rock and ice in order to transfer from one place to another. Whatever it is that happens, it will include a miraculous intervention, much like Moses and the children of Israel when they passed through the narrow passageway in the Red Sea.

And yet it is the factor of *ice* that firmly establishes the setting of this important latter-day event. In addition to prophets smiting the rocks, the scripture specifically says that "the ice will flow down at their presence," pinpointing more than any other locality where this supernatural occurrence will take place.

It has long been a matter of wonderment, as well as skepticism, that the ten tribes might have settled somewhere in an arctic zone, yet a more likely conclusion, once again, might be that such a northern area was merely an embarkation point. This also suggests that it was not only here that the tribes disappeared but in this same kind of area in the future that they will return.

Conditions like these, therefore, refute the idea that the tribes who left Assyria and migrated toward the north eventually diffused among the nations, except for those who might have separated from the main group along the way. To the contrary, the scriptural account definitely implies some other geographical situation or location, one that would provide seclusion for an extended period of time.

This in turn supplements the statement that prophets would "no longer stay themselves" but eventually upon receiving some type of signal would initiate a movement uniting them and their group with normal society. The implication is that a migration "to the outside," as it were, had long been pending, and now with the revelation to proceed, there would be no reason for further delay. The place from which the tribes will be coming remains a mystery, of course, but as to their final place of exit, the reference to falling ice is a primary clue.

Then finally there is the *highway* to be "cast up in the midst of the great deep." Along with the factors of rock and ice, this is the third condition and event that is scheduled to occur just prior to the tribes beginning the last part of their journey, not northward this time but in the opposite direction toward the south.

And whereas some would interpret such a highway figuratively or symbolically, associating it only with a *way of holiness* or the *straight and narrow path*, there is also the more literal interpretation. Especially if the incidents pertaining to rock and ice are viewed as actual occurrences, the one pertaining to the highway needs to be regarded in the same way. When the lost tribes return, in other words, there will be an actual physical event where some kind of roadway is raised up out of the water, no less miraculous than the Israelite passageway across the Red Sea.

Yet still there are those who prefer a less controversial point of view, people with *a tendency to explain away in literal simplicity what they do not wish to understand.* A good example is certainly that pertaining to the ten tribes. Many believe their return will basically be no different from the general gathering of Israel already taking place in which people are assembling in designated areas throughout the world. It is unnecessary, they say, and even inappropriate, to continue looking for the return of an unknown body of people from some mysterious whereabouts.

But such is definitely not the message of the twin verses of scripture in the Doctrine and Covenants. In these two verses alone there is the announcement of a coming event that not only needs to be accepted as fact but also anticipated as an important sign of the times. Surely it is one of the outstanding events yet to come, including the building of temples in Jerusalem and the City of Zion, along with the historic meeting and convocation at Adam-ondi-Ahman. And whether or not it occurs before or after the Second Coming and the Millennium, its status still remains the same. It will indeed be an extraordinary and miraculous event and one of the most unusual occurrences ever to take place during the world's history!

The Books of Nephi

There are other scriptural clues pertaining to the lost tribes, in addition to those in the Doctrine and Covenants, which can be found in *The Book of Mormon*, a record originally inscribed on metal plates and translated by Joseph Smith. In the 22nd chapter of the First Book of Nephi, for example, it states that shortly after 600 B.C. there were many of the House of Israel who were lost from the knowledge of those living in Jerusalem. "Yea, the more part of all the tribes have been led away," the scripture says, "and they are scattered to and fro upon the isles of the sea; and whither they are none of us knoweth, save that we know that they have been led away."[55]

Reference to *isles of the sea* in this context means not just islands but more particularly continents and other land areas as well. Also the people involved were Israelites taken from all of the tribes, including those from Transjordan and northern and central Palestine, and a century or so later additional ones from the southern Kingdom of Judah.

But the most important scriptures in the Book of Mormon which relate specifically to the ten tribes are those recorded in what is called Third Nephi. It is here that the hidden dwelling place of the tribes is specifically mentioned and declared to be an area of remoteness and seclusion. Moreover, it is emphasized that this particular group was led to a private place by God himself, rather than being unsupervised and settling in an area on their own.

In regard to the tribes in general, Jesus remarked on one occasion that he had never told any of the people in Jerusalem about those which had been taken away. "Neither at any time hath the Father given me a commandment," he said, "that I should tell unto them concerning the other tribes of the House of Israel whom the Father hath led away out of the land." It was because of waywardness in the original group, he said, that others had been separated from among them.

Those he was addressing at the time were Israelites themselves, people whose ancestors six hundred years before the time of Christ had left the city of Jerusalem and migrated to the American Continent. They had developed into a large nation and were now contemporary not only with those in Jerusalem but with a third group somewhere in the north who were the lost tribes.

"But now I go unto the Father," Jesus told them, "and also to show myself unto the lost tribes of Israel, for they are not lost unto the Father, for he knoweth where he hath taken them."[56]

Although these scriptures might be interpreted privately in more than one way, still the material which they contain is enough to provide some definite information: (1) The "other tribes of the house of Israel," those who were not living in Jerusalem or on the American Continent, were residing somewhere distantly as a separate group or nation. (2) Their whereabouts was unknown except to the Father, and indeed it was he who had led them there in the first place. (3) The lost tribes received the gospel when Jesus ministered unto them, or very possibly even earlier, and by implication from the Doctrine and Covenants they from time to time had prophets among them.

Consequently, such statements provide the type of subject matter which further warrants the idea that the ten tribes are an exclusive and unusual group, located in an area where their existence and living conditions might be relatively different from those of people in regular society. Because of this it is very possible that they escaped being dispersed and sifted among non-Israelite people and down through the ages retained a pure strain of lineage and ancestry.

Had they remained strictly in the north country and eventually occupied any number of surrounding areas, their group at the time of Christ would probably have been associated with the large barbaric population known as the Germanic tribes. This would make them contemporary with such groups as the Huns, Vandals, and Goths, as these people were later called, and likely they were already being diffused throughout the nations.

Yet at the same time, if the latter is true, there would definitely be a problem as far as the visitation of Christ is concerned. To say that he visited people who had intermingled with Germanic tribes, in other words, and organized his church among them, would be inconsistent with what is recorded in the Bible. This is evidenced in a statement made by Jesus at one time when he said he had been sent to teach only those who were strictly Israelites, which in the particular area of Palestine meant people whose ancestors formerly were of the Kingdom of Judah and had generally stayed separate from outside lineages.

"I am not sent," he said, "but unto the lost sheep of the house of Israel."[57]

It is significant that this statement did not include people in the cities of nearby Samaria, many of whom were part Israelite but through intermarriage had become mixed with other religious and ethnic groups. To his apostles, in fact, he specifically gave instructions to stay away from such areas.

"Go not into the way of the Gentiles," he told them, "and into any city of the Samaritans enter ye not: but go rather to the lost sheep of the house of Israel."[58] Jesus was adamant on this point, and it was not until after his death and resurrection that the gospel teachings were taken to other groups of people

In regard to populations north and northeast of what was then known as the Roman Empire, therefore, some of whom have been considered to be the ten tribes that the Lord visited after he left the American Continent, there is definitely the problem pertaining to Israelite ancestry. Obviously it would be inconsistent for Jesus to bypass the Samaritans in Palestine and at the same time visit Israelites further to the north who by now had inter-married with other people and were at least partially dispersed among Germanic tribes.

Rather a more logical circumstance and conclusion might be that the tribes had originally gone to a more distant location where they could definitely be separate from "the multitude of the nations." Such a place would give them the privacy and seclusion necessary in order to work out their particular destiny, whatever that might have been. In addition, it would enable them to maintain their status as "lost sheep of the house of Israel." And then in connection with this, after many centuries of iso-lation, there would be their predicted restoration and the remarkable circumstances of their return, the miraculous resolution of things at which time rocks would crumble and ice would fall, and a highway would be raised up "in the midst of the great deep" pointing the way south-ward to a new life and destination and the brand new city called Zion!

A Question of Identity

An important motive of the ten tribes in going into the north country, according to the Apocrypha, was to find a place where they could keep the religious statues and commandments which they had not previously observed. This means that it was a religious movement more than anything else, although there were undoubtedly political, economic, and social factors as well.

Those making the journey had never been to Palestine, yet their history and ancestral background very likely predisposed them to a place where they could keep livestock and raise crops, bring up children in a more controlled environment, and maybe build another temple. It was also important for them and their posterity to marry within their own group. Obeying God's commandments, in other words, which included the Mosaic Law, was uppermost in their minds, and finding the right place to settle was a primary factor.

It is impossible to say how many of the Israelites in Assyria, if any, had already intermarried with foreign colonists. There were undoubtedly some who had established cultural and social ties and later preferred not to leave. On the other hand, the ones who did belong to the final group were possibly descendants of people who had never intermarried at all but had kept their Israelite lineage intact. Tobit and his son Tobias would be good examples.

Again a significant aspect of the ten tribes migrating to the north is that they were most likely a very exclusive group. Their purpose had been predetermined, and by arrangement they were to be guided by God himself. It was he who would take them to an unidentified place that had been prepared for them, after which they literally would become lost to the knowledge of the world. Their circumstances and whereabouts would remain completely unknown, and yet they would not be "lost unto the Father," Jesus would say at a later time, "for he knoweth where he hath taken them."[59]

The idea of seclusion and isolation, therefore, continued to be an important factor. As late as six hundred years after they left Assyria, during the time of Christ's ministry in Palestine, the tribes were still hidden in some area related to the north country.

It was important also for them to continue the policy of pure Israelite citizenship. Only be being completely separate from other nations, preserving their particular character and identity, could they do this. Because of a previous election and calling in preexistence, their Israelite lineage possessed a preferred status, as it were, which consequently made them an integral part of those who were designated as *lost sheep of the house of Israel.*

And yet while this is true, it did not guarantee any of the Israelites immunity from waywardness and transgression. To the contrary, such people were sometimes just as affected by negative forces as those who lived around them. Although they had inherited a predisposition toward truth and righteousness in comparison with other nations, history showed repeatedly that it was nevertheless easy for them to be otherwise.

The Israelites who lived anciently on the American Continent, for example, were often a belligerent group and warred with one another. The same was true to some extent with those in the kingdoms of Israel and Judah. The most glaring instance and contradiction of all, of

THE TEN LOST TRIBES

course, was when the Jewish people in Jerusalem con-
victed and crucified Jesus Christ.

But all of this to the side, the idea in the beginning
was still that the House of Israel was a unique and special people, "a peculiar treasure" unto the Lord, "a kingdom of priests and an holy nation."[60] Unlike any other
group, it was an organization that was meant to be a positive and stabilizing influence throughout the world, one
that would serve as an ensign to the nations and be the
medium through which all people of the earth would
be blessed.

And this one aspect alone, if nothing else, relates
significantly to the ten tribes. It could be, in fact, that
they were established for the very purpose of seeing if at
least one group of Israelites could succeed in fulfilling a
peculiar destiny. In a way, they would be representative
of all the tribes, testing the process of everyday living in
a new location and a new set of circumstances to see if
the original concept of Israel could be effected and brought
about. In this way also there would be a more meaning-
ful differentiation between a part of the ten tribes on the
one hand and the rest of Israel on the other.

The belief has often been stated that there will not
only be a *literal gathering of Israel* in the last days but
a *restoration of the ten tribes* as well. Yet to say that all
segments of the tribes are currently dispersed among the
nations and living together as a group is tantamount
to saying that it is mainly Israel in general that will be
gathered.

A more definitive statement would be that there are
specifically two separate peoples involved and that the
lost tribes, wherever they are and under whatever conditions they might be living, are definitely aside from the
rest of Israel. Otherwise a well-known article of faith
might be restated as a belief in "the literal gathering and

restoration of Israel including the ten tribes," which obviously would sound out of place and redundant, considering the intended meaning.

Once again it is the idea of people explaining away in simple terms what they do not wish to understand. It is much easier for them, in other words, to conceive of a gathering of Israel, including the lost tribes, that is closer to a more conventional belief. In this way they can bypass the skepticism and criticism which traditionally are part of an unorthodox point of view.

But in taking this kind of approach, there also might be considerable risk, namely settling for something that is simple and generic in lieu of an alternative that is more complex but true. And although this kind of situation actually does exist, it is nevertheless a chance and possible consequence that many people seem willing to take!

Return of the Tribes

If the concept is true that the lost tribes exist somewhere as a partially identifiable group, separate and apart from the nations, and that someday they will reappear amid circumstances of rock, ice, and water, another important idea is the approximate time of their future return. Will they come *before* the beginning of the Millennium, for example, or will it be *after*? Also in regard to specific events, will they arrive prior to the Battle of Armageddon and the holocaust of fire that will cleanse the earth or sometime following it?

Undoubtedly there are pros and cons to such a question, and like the time of the Second Coming only one person maybe knows the answer. And yet certain clues and arguments might be given to support the idea that the tribes will return at a time *before* the fire and Millennium ever begin.

One of the more significant clues is the relationship of their return to the building of the City of Zion in western Missouri, the city to which the ten tribes will come soon after their reappearance. The idea is that before the city is constructed, along with its extensive temple complex, certain things need to be accomplished, such as acquiring and preparing the land and providing building materials and labor, all of which will be a mammoth project. In addition, there is also the possibility that political upheaval and civil unrest will accompany such preparations, or at least precede or follow them.

It is probable, in other words, that the situation in the United States at that time will be radically different from what it is today. The implications are that the country will become considerably less populated than at present and that not only riots and crime will be more prevalent but also such things as drought, a disrupted economy, and natural disasters. Certainly one of the most pointed comments on this subject is one made by Joseph Smith in a letter written to an editor in the year 1833. One remark especially contains a highly significant reference to domestic conditions and the future return of the lost tribes.

> "And now I am prepared to say," he said, "by the authority of Jesus Christ, that not many years shall pass away before the United States shall present such a scene of bloodshed as has not a parallel in the history of our nation; pestilence, hail, famine, and earthquake will sweep the wicked of this generation from off the face of the land, to open and prepare the way for the return of the lost tribes of Israel from the north country.[61]

This particular statement, coming from the man who translated the Book of Mormon and brought forth the revelations contained in the Doctrine and Covenants, is extremely important in establishing a correct date for the restoration of the ten tribes. It suggests strongly that their return will be *prior* to the commencement of the Millennium instead of *after*, at a time when conditions in the United States will have greatly deteriorated but eventually improved enough for the tribes to return.

A further implication is that these people, possibly a tremendous host not unlike those anciently who came out of Egypt, will be reinstated to a normal status in society in preparation for the coming of Christ. This means they will witness this great latter-day event instead of missing it and in company with other righteous inhabitants of the earth be caught up to meet the Lord when he comes.

Placing the arrival of the tribes *before* the beginning of the Millennium and the holocaust of fire definitely gives credence to the idea that a preliminary cleansing will be needed to open up the way and prepare the land, not just for the tribes to return but possibly for the building of a city and temple as well. It is just one of several things necessary to make way for the Second Coming. Subsequent to this latter event, in fact, everything will be anticlimactic, the earth and heavens already having been renewed and all things resolved pertaining to the human family and the Kingdom of God.

But in the meantime, and in addition to Joseph Smith's 1833 prediction, there are other clues which provide important information and help to establish a correct time frame. These again are provided by the 133rd section of the Doctrine and Covenants where it tells about the ten tribes journeying southward following their exit through a mass of rock and ice and the traversal over a miraculous highway.

"Their enemies shall become a prey unto them," the record says, "and in the barren deserts there shall come forth pools of living water; and the parched ground shall no longer be a thirsty land."[62]

Certainly it is possible to use symbolism or other representations in interpreting such scriptures, but anything short of a literal meaning again runs the risk of substituting a less valid explanation. This does not exclude certain figurative aspects, which in all likelihood are present, yet in regard to the migrating tribes of Israel, it is reasonable to assume that an actual physical journey across the land is being described.

It appears that the conditions involved, in other

words, are pre-Millennial rather than those which would exist at a later time. The idea especially that there will be enemies of the tribes sounds like a condition occurring at an earlier date rather than a later one.

Finally at the time of the Second Coming, there will be an entirely new situation in the world, and vast changes will take place on the earth's surface. Besides widespread burning, geographic and geologic occurrences will also occur. It is difficult to imagine what the extent of these events will be, but in the Doctrine and Covenants there is at least a partial description.

The Lord will speak from the City of Zion and also from Jerusalem, the scriptures say, "and his voice shall be heard among all people; and it shall be a voice as of the voice of many waters, and as the voice of a great thunder, which shall break down the mountains, and the valleys shall not be found.

> He shall command the great deep, and it shall be driven back into the north countries, and the islands shall become one land; and the land of Jerusalem and the land of Zion shall be turned back into their own place, and the earth shall be like as it was in the days before it was divided.[63]

As the oceans and seas are altered and surface water is greatly reduced, the landmass of the earth will become one gigantic continent. Bodies of water will still be present but nothing in comparison to what exists today. And as a consequence, these geographic aspects alone suggest a time schedule for the return of the ten tribes. The physical conditions associated with their arrival, for example, again suggest a period preceding the catastrophic occurrences and changes of the Second Coming instead of one following them.

Also there is the matter of 144,000 missionaries

mentioned in the Book of Revelation, men who in the last days will stand with Jesus on Mount Zion and have "his Father's name written in their foreheads." These people, according to an explanation in the Doctrine and Covenants, are high priests whose mission in latter times will be to teach the gospel and "bring as many as will come to the church of the Firstborn."[64]

The thing that makes this latter-day group relevant is that it will consist of twelve thousand men from each of the Israelite tribes and will be selected "out of every nation, kindred, tongue, and people by the angels to whom is given power over the nations of the earth."[65] Again their special calling and assignment will be to do missionary work. And although the time involved is questionable, as to whether it will be before or after the Second Coming, or both, the question of timing in relation to the return of the lost tribes is a significant one.

It is possible, in other words, that a considerable number of the 144,000 will be selected from the returning tribes themselves, especially if they have been in isolation down through the centuries and have retained a pure Israelite lineage. Others will undoubtedly come from those who have been diffused among the nations, although the identity of most of these people, except for the descendants of Ephraim and Judah, has so far remained almost completely unknown. In the end, however, all of the tribes except Dan will be involved, resulting in a combined force of kindred Israelites heretofore unknown in the history of the world.

Indeed, the work of these special latter-day missionaries, representing for the first time all of the House of Israel together, will be a unique and extraordinary event that will be a primary force in preparing for the historic Millennium!

Importance of Ephraim

If anyone were to be singled out from all of Israel's tribes, based on notability and standing in the Bible, it would probably be either Judah or Joseph, the latter being represented also by his two sons Ephraim and Manasseh. Yet in relation to latter times and the events preceding the Millennium, it is the name of Ephraim that definitely is most prominent. Anciently it was Ephraim and his posterity that exerted a significant influence in the affairs of the House of Israel, and it is many of his descendants today who are allegedly doing the same thing.

In the beginning, however, things started out in a much different way. It was Reuben, the oldest of Jacob's sons, who occupied the position of prestige and authority. By reason of the birthright, he had the opportunity to be the renowned leader among all of those who were called Israelites. But Reuben transgressed a law and broke an important commandment, and the birthright was given to another, not to the next in line according to a usual type of seniority but to Joseph along with Ephraim and Manasseh.

Then after a time, and for whatever reason, the main part of the birthright eventually passed exclusively to Ephraim. He and his lineage, in turn, were set apart for a special purpose, one pertaining to the period of time before and during the *scattering of Israel*, and more importantly to the period later known as the *gathering*, the climactic years leading up to the end of the world's first historical period and the beginning of the Millennium.

It is in this modern era, in fact, as the world's current history draws to a close, that the name of Ephraim has again come to the forefront. Subscribing to a Mormon point of view, people of Israelite ancestry, and especially those who descend from this one man, are assembling in thousands of places worldwide, accepting the idea that Israel is now being gathered in preparation for the Second Coming and that the ten tribes, by whatever process, will one day be restored to their former place in society. In addition, they espouse a very different kind of doctrine, including higher ordinances of the gospel performed in temples and also modern revelation such as that contained in the Book of Mormon and the Book of Doctrine and Covenants.

But it is the belief in a modern-day Israel, marked by an unusual affinity to Ephraim, that especially sets these people apart as a unique church and religious organization. A belief in the restoration of the ten tribes in particular is a distinguishing characteristic.

When the lost tribes return, for example, and travel southward to the City of Zion, they will be received there by fellow Israelites referred to in scripture as the "children of Ephraim." This will not be their final destination, but it is here that they will obtain an important religious endowment consisting of ordinances pertaining to the temple and possibly also their portion of the assignment reserved for the 144,000 who will preach the gospel in connection with the Second Coming. On Mount Zion, another name for the city, this latter group will eventually stand with Jesus himself as they assist him in ushering in the Millennium.

"And there shall they fall down and be crowned with glory," referring to the ten tribes, "even in Zion, by the hands of the servants of the Lord, even the children of Ephraim. And they shall be filled with songs of everlasting joy.

"Behold, this is the blessing of the everlasting God upon the tribes of Israel, and the richer blessing upon the head of Ephraim and his fellows."

Also concerning the 144,000 missionaries, the scripture says that an angel will fly through the midst of heaven with an extraordinary message.

> Prepare ye the way of the Lord, and make his paths straight, for the hour of his coming is nigh, when the Lamb shall stand upon Mount Zion, and with him a hundred and forty-four thousand, having his Father's name written on their foreheads.[66]

An important aspect of these events, of course, is that the authority inherent in the tribe of Ephraim will also very possibly be present among those returning from the north country, as it will be with those in the City of Zion. As it was in the Kingdom of Israel prior to Assyrian captivity, so it could be that Ephraim of the ten tribes will continue to exercise its part of the ancient birthright.

It would be Ephraim on the one hand, in other words, assisting Ephraim on the other in further establishing the Kingdom of God on earth. Two important segments of the same tribe would once more join together. Just as the former had exerted leadership and authority during pre-captivity days, and logically all down through succeeding centuries, so might they in latter times again fill that important role and calling. Their position and standing would be subordinate to a more prominent leadership in Zion but nevertheless would represent a highly significant force.

And if things do happen that way, the authority given to Ephraim anciently will once more be renewed and reconfirmed. In the tradition of Joseph of Egypt who was a savior and benefactor to his people, the power vested in the son will be a continuing influence in the affairs of the kingdom. As in days of old, his name and leadership will still be foremost among his peers. Then as the time draws near for the Second Coming and the commencement of the Millennium, it will definitely be those among the tribe of Ephraim who will be in the forefront!

The Land of the North

When the lost tribes return from their long season of isolation, they will be coming from a nondescript area known as the *north countries* or *land of the north.* It is also to this same region, and very possibly by no coincidence, that the *waters of the great deep* will be driven at the time of the Second Coming.

These two momentous events, occurring very closely together in time and in the same part of the globe, constitute an extremely unusual circumstance, each event implying something important and unique about the other. One will be coming from an isolated and undisclosed place, in other words, while the other is mysteriously disappearing in the same area.

As the waters of the great deep, presumably a major part of the Atlantic and Pacific Oceans along with adjacent seas, are "driven" toward the north and relocated, there will necessarily have to be some kind of alteration or adjustment of sea level. Obviously water will not pile up in the north countries but theoretically be directed to some other location. Also it is in this same general area that the lost tribes will appear, rock and ice falling down before them and a highway rising out of the sea.

These events will not occur simultaneously but will be near enough in time to give significant meaning to the geographic setting of the north country. Indeed it seems more than a coincidence that the time and place involved are relatively the same. As a consequence, the implication is very strong that an extraordinary phenomenon will be taking place, one that establishes an interesting relationship between the two occurrences.

Certain aspects of this relationship have to do with water and its unusual capacity to be driven toward the north, a giant flood apparently being relocated to a new location. This in turn raises some important questions. If the earth's sea level is lowered, for example, creating a single gigantic landmass, where will the surplus water go? Will it be relocated according to a process of rising and sinking terrain, or will large volumes of sea and ocean just miraculously disappear? Or is there a third possibility that water will actually "be gathered together unto one place" and then be engineered hydraulically into subterranean areas of the earth? Are there so-called "fountains of the deep," in other words, that can absorb tremendous amounts of water into underground reservoirs?

This last concept in particular, like others in the past, might be regarded as unlikely by members of the scientific community, as well as by people in general, yet as things turn out, it could conceivably be closer to the truth than any other theory! Justification for such is found in the first chapter of Genesis in the Bible where it states that during the Creation, water was gathered together causing dry land to appear. Moreover, the wording involved is that the water was specifically accumulated to one place.

> And God said, Let the waters under the heaven be gathered together unto one place, and let the dry land appear: and it was so.[67]

Reference to *one place,* of course, could mean that all of the water ended up in one area and the land in another, yet there is also a second interpretation, or at least a double meaning. An example of this is again found in the Doctrine and Covenants where it says that sometime in the future, a huge volume of ocean will be drawn to a specific geographical location in the north, after which a uniform sea level, by some type of natural phenomenon, will apparently be reestablished and maintained.

"He shall command the great deep," the scripture says, referring to the Lord and his Second Coming, "and it shall be driven back into the north countries, and the islands shall become one land."

The terminology of water being "driven back into the north" suggests that that is where the water originated in the first place, discounting at the same time the idea of rising and sinking terrain or instantaneous evaporation. It is a matter of water moving supernaturally in a northerly direction to a point where in some way it literally disappears, thus reducing the remaining volume of ocean to a uniform sea level.

In this regard, there is the additional scriptural explanation pertaining to a single continent and landmass. "And the land of Jerusalem and the land of Zion shall be turned back into their own place, and the earth shall be like as it was in the days before it was divided."[68]

The division referred to is the biblical event in the days of Peleg in which an increased sea level apparently resulted in the present-day arrangement of islands and continents. Prior to that time, assuming that the occurrence in Peleg's time was indeed a separate event, there were two other floods, one during the days of Noah and also the inundation of the earth at the time of Creation. All three of these occurrences had similar characteristics and might well have taken place by way of water coming mainly out of the north country, destined later to return to the same place.

In conclusion, therefore, there is also the matter of the ten tribes disappearing and reappearing in the northern part of the globe, events no less significant than the periodic appearance and disappearance of gigantic floods. The possibility of subterranean reservoirs, in fact, where the earth's deluges originate and later return, definitely furnishes an important clue and possible solution as to where the tribes went so many years ago and how for all of these centuries they have been able to remain in isolation.

The implications are there, at least, suggesting that somewhere in relation to the earth and in connection with the north country, the lost tribes of Israel do exist today as a separate body of people. They have not been mysteriously removed, as were those in the ancient city of Enoch, nor are they residing on some other planet or sphere. Rather the likelihood is that they are still somewhere within the earth's structure and organization and will someday rejoin regular society according to the time and manner predicted.

Like the darkening of the sun and moon and the falling of stars from heaven, this event will likewise be accompanied by miraculous phenomena and circumstances and surely will be one of the final signs of the times, showing that the start of the Millennium is imminent and that events immediately preceding have already begun!

A Place of Seclusion

There appears to be no possibility of discussing the return of the lost tribes of Israel in a simple and realistic way. Especially in light of scriptural clues, anything less than a supernatural explanation would probably be too commonplace and generic.

The one reference in scripture, in fact, that applies to the tribes' return, specifically lists three conditions or circumstances that will be present, all of which are supernatural. (1) Prophets leading the tribes will smite the rocks, presumably some kind of obstruction or barrier. (2) Ice will flow down before them. (3) Some type of highway will miraculously "be cast up in the midst" of a sea or ocean.

> And they who are in the north countries shall come in remembrance before the Lord; and their prophets shall hear his voice, and shall no longer stay themselves; and they shall smite the rocks, and the ice shall flow down at their presence. And an highway shall be cast up in the midst of the great deep.[69]

Any attempt to clarify or minimize the impact of this unusual description will very possibly be tantamount to wrestling the scriptures. In this account especially, it is important to accept the scripture for what it actually says, at the same time acknowledging the possibility that in the written material following it, there might be a certain amount of symbolism and figurative expression.

But in regard to the three conditions or circumstances pertaining to the tribes and their return, namely those of rock, ice, and water, the language expressed is explicitly clear, not just in describing the manner in which the tribes will appear but hinting very strongly at the place or region from which they will be coming!

In order to approach any kind of understanding concerning the present whereabouts of the lost tribes, however, it is necessary first to look at another instance in which supernatural conditions exist. The *Spirit World*, for example, the place where all people go after death, is reputed to be somewhere within the actual confines of the earth. It is not in heaven or in any other place in the universe, but rather at some location relative to the earth itself.

This is a belief espoused by the Mormon Church, and like so many other of its tenets, it requires the use of both faith and intellect. It is the same type of requirement as that involved in accepting the principle of the resurrection, as well as many of the miracles that Jesus performed as part of his ministry.

A further belief is that the earth was created not only as a place of mortal existence, as well as a temporary habitation for the spirits of those who have died, but as a future place in the hereafter for people who obey the laws of God and keep his commandments. In other words, it will one day actually become a part of *heaven*. Again this is Mormon philosophy, yet theoretically it pertains to anyone who can develop a certain kind of spirituality and qualify for a high level of living. It is the concept of people acquiring not just immortality but celestial life as well, in the process of which the earth will eventually be celestialized and become their permanent residence.

The planet earth, in the meantime, according to this

same philosophy, remains an exceptionally unusual place. In essence, it is presently accommodating two sets of lives going on at the same time, one group in mortality and the other somewhere in an unknown area called the Spirit World. On the one hand is a normal physical existence while on the other is one that is supernatural and difficult to explain, although nevertheless in some way directly associated with the earth.

In comparison with the latter, the same also might be true in regard to the lost tribes of Israel. Because of extremely unusual conditions and circumstances, both they and people in the Spirit World are apparently living in a different type of existence, enveloped in almost complete mystery and uncertainty with no accurate explanation as to where they might be. Each is easily a matter of speculation and controversy. But the important fact is that they do exist, and somewhere their lives are taking place concurrently. The puzzling question is where!

During the hours between the death of Jesus and his resurrection, he spent at least some of that time in what the Bible refers to as the *heart of the earth*. This is an area which has been associated with the Spirit World.

"For Christ also hath once suffered for sins," the scripture says, "the just for the unjust, that he might bring us to God, being put to death in the flesh, but quickened by the Spirit: by which also he went and preached unto the spirits in prison."[70]

> For as Jonas was three days and three nights in the whale's belly, so shall the Son of Man be three days and three nights in the heart of the earth.[71]

Of course, other interpretations might be given to the "heart of the earth," but at least it does suggest a certain location somewhere within the earth's physical make-up and organization. Wherever it is, there are people there who are alive and who have already passed from mortality.

As to a similar location, the same also might be true of the lost tribes. At an undisclosed place in relation to the earth, they are currently going through what has to be considered a supernatural type of existence, albeit one still of mortality. They are not residing as a people dispersed among the nations, as commonly supposed, but are living more exclusively as a separate group and nation by themselves. The existing circumstances are necessarily different, but at the same time their manner of living might possibly differ very little from that of people in general.

Consequently, the situation in which they exist results in a concept that is understandably difficult to believe. Surely it is one that is not readily accepted or understood. Even in a modern age of discovery, where science has produced technology that half a century ago would have been regarded only as science fiction, it is something more likely to be rejected at first than accepted. And yet at the same time, the type of public reaction involved is not without significant precedence in the Bible.

When Mary Magdalene approached the apostles that Sunday morning, for example, and told them she had seen Jesus alive, their initial reaction was not one of elation and belief. Instead they were very disbelieving, discounting what she said as "idle tales." In spite of all the miraculous things they had seen while accompanying Jesus in his ministry, this was one thing pertaining to the supernatural they could not accept.

Nor was it to their discredit in reacting as they did. Such a thing as the resurrection had never happened before, and for a person to disbelieve rather than believe was only what might have been expected. The apostles soon learned through experience that it was true, however, and for them the idle tales and an improbable concept quickly became reality.

Much the same also might be true with the ten tribes. Whereas they are now shrouded in mystery and controversy, their alleged status ranging from contemporary society to situations extraterrestrial, the truth about them will one day become known. Theories and speculation will then quickly disappear, and it is not unlikely on that occasion that people will accept all that has happened not only as a remarkable event but a supernatural one as well.

The evidence, in fact, actually suggests that the lost tribes of Israel are presently living in a locality not *on the earth,* but somewhere *in the earth,* whatever that particular reference comes to mean. Also their eventual emergence from such a place in the future will require the smiting of rocks and the removal of ice, along with a highway exiting by way of the sea. These are the conditions outlined in scripture and at present the only facts available. Everything else is conjecture and speculation.

As a consequence, an interaction of intellect with both faith and imagination is required in responding to this kind of situation. Certainly it involves a very specific kind of rationalization. As with a belief in the Spirit World and the resurrection, it is first the ability to visualize, then to conceptualize, and finally as far as faith is concerned to actualize, taking the facts and evidence into consideration and forming an opinion and a conviction.

In relation to the lost tribes, this does *not* require a resort to science fiction or some imaginative journey to the center of the earth. The so-called hollow earth theories which have often been publicized are not an accurate or relevant concept. But an acceptance of an "in the earth" location for the tribes nevertheless *does* require an acknowledgment of certain supernatural conditions, another "heart of the earth," for example, or some comparable region.

Obviously, in associating a large group of people with circumstances pertaining to rock, ice, and water, there will have to be a geographic and geologic setting different from anything commonplace or conventional. Everything definitely suggests some type of condition in another department of the earth, an area capable of accommodating a relatively large civilization of people and keeping them hidden from the world for more than twenty-five centuries. The implication is that something far from the ordinary is involved.

And it is here that a discussion becomes even more difficult, if not impossible at times, in explaining things with reasonable credibility. It is also at this point that the matter needs to be stated exactly and unequivocally. To describe a theoretical situation as it actually might exist, in other words, is to say that the lost tribes of Israel, by way of some type of supernatural phenomena, are located somewhere *beneath the surface of the earth*, not deep in the interior as advocated by the hollow earth theories but in an upper portion pertaining to the crust and mantle. Unlike the Spirit World, their existence is still one of mortality, although at the same time one where normal conditions have necessarily been modified in order to accommodate an extraordinary situation and a unique group of people.

Such is a very candid explanation, and even though is not an easy concept to accept, still it is one that is compatible and reconcilable with the implications of *rock, ice, and water*, the incontrovertible conditions associated with the tribes and their future return.[72] Moreover, there appears to be no other way of viewing these people as an independent body, free from intermixture with the nations, and at the same time keeping them in an area associated with the north country.

In support of such a theory there is also the extraordinary reference in scripture to the "waters of the great deep" and the idea that much of the seas and oceans will someday "be driven back into the north countries," there to disappear and be redistributed. This involves the possibility that the reason water is amassed in a northern region, in the first place, is so it can be directed hydraulically into a subterranean area.

A similar event could have happened during the creation of the earth when God said, "Let the waters under the heaven be gathered together unto one place," and also during the Great Flood when "the waters returned from off the earth." In both cases floodwater presumably returned to the so-called "fountains of the deep" where, at least in Noah's time, most of it had originated.[73]

Although the "in the earth" theory concerning the ten tribes is a challenging one, therefore, it ultimately might be the only one that relates meaningfully to the concept of global floods, as well as to the unusual way that the tribes will come out of the *north countries*. As in other instances, the key insight into the solution of a problem is again associated with only very brief passages of scripture.

In addition, there are still the continuing questions pertaining to huge volumes of water during a large flood. Where do they come from, for example, and to what place do they return? How reasonable is it to assume that huge underground reservoirs exist beneath the surface of the earth? In the days of Noah, it took five months for floodwater to appear and another five to disappear, which suggests a vast subterranean area. Similarly at the time of the Second Coming, when much of the sea and ocean is relocated to the north, several weeks or months might again be involved.

Yet the important question is not what happens to the floods when they are over but how this relates to the lost tribes, their present circumstances and location. What correlation is there, if any, between water disappearing in the north countries and the ten tribes reappearing in the same area? Certainly this is not just a coincidence but rather an unusual phenomenon that has significant implications.

Again it intimates very strongly that somewhere beneath the earth's surface in the northern hemisphere, there is a mammoth repository for water. From this area, water initially flooded the globe during the period of Creation and then returned to its source when it was "gathered together unto one place." Many centuries later it reemerged and then again receded at the conclusion of the Flood, as well as possibly reappearing a third time on the occasion of the earth being divided in the days of Peleg. A definite pattern was always present, in other words, and it is one that offers a possible solution to the question pertaining to the lost tribes.

Theoretically it suggests that a huge subterranean area of water, existing below the earth's surface somewhere in the mantle or crust, is adjacent to a large land area which by way of supernatural conditions is accommodating a civilization of people. In the same way that a population of 125 million is able to subsist on 146,000 square miles in present-day Japan, so a comparable number of people, or possibly much less, according to unknown laws and principles, might be living on the same amount of territory in another part of the earth's structure. Factors such as those relating to light source and atmospheric conditions would necessarily be subject to a very different set of principles, of course. Yet it is possible! And although such a theory at first seems incredible and unbelievable, even preposterous or ridiculous compared to normal ways of thinking, the evidence nevertheless does point in the direction of just such a place!

Moreover, in connection with this idea there are at least seven kinds of supporting evidence. First, the theory keeps the tribes in the right region of the globe, namely the north country. Second, it links their traveling and existence with the important aspect of water. Third, it involves the interaction of rock, ice, and water in regard to a point of exit, and possibly also a previous place of entrance. Fourth, it gives additional meaning to certain scriptures that refer to things *under or beneath the earth*. Fifth, it is part of a historical pattern or cycle which implies that the tribes disappeared in much the same way that someday they will reappear. Sixth, the idea gains significant credibility from the parallel existence of the Spirit World.

And finally there is logic in the thought that the tribes actually had no other place to go. Since they were last known to be in the north country, allegedly not diffusing among the nations but traveling together as a group, they either had to go *up*, so to speak, or to go *down*. To go up suggests a situation similar to those who disappeared from the ancient City of Enoch, a possibility discounted because the two situations are so different. To go down, on the other hand, although the idea is unorthodox and revolutionary, appears to be a more likely occurrence, even though it raises almost insurmountable questions.

The thought also keeps coming back that any solution relating to the lost tribes of Israel, if it is to be reconciled with the little information that exists, will probably have to involve the unexpected and the supernatural. Very few of the clues mentioned in scripture are ordinary or commonplace. Consequently, there is no easy way of visualizing where these people are located right now or explaining the miraculous circumstances which have been predicted for their return. Only one thing appears to be certain.

And that is that wherever the tribes are located and whatever their conditions and circumstances might be, all that eventually happens will take place somewhere within the confines of the earth. Everything relating to earth life and mortality, in fact, and much also that is immortality, will continue to remain centered on this one particular planet.

Certainly in the overall scope of things, the earth is a very remarkable place with the potential of accommodating any number of extraordinary situations, the most notable of which is the Spirit World. Yet two other possible situations also exist, those of large subterranean reservoirs of water beneath the earth's surface and a nearby locality containing the lost tribes. These last two in particular, as far as present-day society is concerned, undoubtedly are among the most important.

This means that the coming and going of gigantic volumes of water, occurring at strategic times during the world's history, very possibly contain the missing clues and information as to where the lost tribes are located. These floods, the culmination of which will one day be part of a dramatic climax and denouement at the time of the Second Coming and the beginning of the Millennium, are scheduled to end during the same general time period when the tribes make their dramatic reappearance. Both will occur at a historic intersection of events and circumstances. And on that occasion, when all things pertaining to the earth's temporal existence become known, surely the truth will finally be revealed about the elusive group of people belonging to the House of Israel who down through the long line of centuries have been such a puzzling enigma and mystery!

References and Comments

Note: The King James Version of the Bible, the Book of Mormon, and the Doctrine Covenants are standard works of The Church of Jesus Christ of Latter-day Saints.

1. Doctrine and Covenants 77:12.
2. Revelation 6:14; 8:1.
3. Doctrine and Covenants 88:95.
4. 2 Peter 3:8; Psalms 90:4.
5. Isaiah 2:3; Micah 4:2.
6. Ezekiel 38:15.
7. Ezekiel 38:4.
8. Joel 2:2–3.
9. Amos 9:9.
10. Doctrine and Covenants 133:26–27.
11. 2 Kings 15:29; 17:5–6; 18:9–11; 1 Chronicles 5:26.
12. Jeremiah 7:15.
13. 2 Kings 15:29; 2 Chronicles 5:26.
14. 2 Kings 17:5–6; 18:9–11.
15. 1 Kings 16:24.
16. J. W. Crowfoot, K. M. Kenyon, and E. L. Sukenik, *The Buildings at Samaria* (London: Palestinian Exploration Fund, 1965), 1.
17. Bob Becking, *The Fall of Samaria, An Historical and Archaeological Study* (Leiden: E. J. Brill, 1992), 1; Andre Parrot, *Samaria, the Capital of the Kingdom of Israel* (New York: Philosophical Library, 1958), 48–52.
18. Ezra 4:2, 9–10; Parrot, *Samaria*, 88.
19. Daniel David Luckenbill, *Ancient Records of Assyria and Babylonia* (Chicago: University of Chicago Press, 1927), 2:3, 27, 70.

20. H. R. Hall, *The Ancient History of the Near East* (London: Methuen & Co., 1957), 474.

21. Bustenay Oded, *Mass Deportations and Deportees in the Neo-Assyrian Empire* (Wiesbaden, Germany: Ludwig Reichert Verlag, 1979), 44, 84–86.

22. 2 Chronicles 30:1, 6.

23. 2 Chronicles 30:25.

24. 2 Chronicles 34:3, 6, 9.

25. James Hastings, ed., *Dictionary of the Bible* (New York: Charles Scribner's Sons, 1963), 364; James Orr, ed., *The International Standard Bible Encyclopedia* (Grand Rapids, Mich.: Wm. B. Eerdman's Publishing Company, 1960), 2:1337.

26. Bruce M. Metzger, ed., *The Apocrypha of the Old Testament, Revised Standard Version* (New York: Oxford University Press, 1965), 65.

27. Oded, *Mass Deportations,* 86.

28. Oded, *Mass Deportations,* 86.

29. Oded, *Mass Deportations,* 70–71.

30. Becking, *Fall of Samaria,* 62–63; Oded, *Mass Deportations,* 92.

31. Metzger, *Apocrypha of the Old Testament,* 65 (2 Esdras 13:41–42).

32. Hall, *Ancient History of the Near East,* 466. Others have also expressed this same view, pointing out that only a part of a conquered area was taken into captivity.

33. Heber C. Snell, *Ancient Israel: Its Study and Meaning* (Salt Lake City: University of Utah Press), 142; Oded, *Mass Deportations,* 22.

34. Oded, *Mass Deportations,* 18; Parrot, *Samaria,* 51. Note: The number of Samarian captives usually mentioned in other texts, and the one that appears to be correct, is 27,290.

35. Oded, *Mass Deportations,* 24, 58.

36. Oded, *Mass Deportations,* 14–15, 79.

37. Parrot, *Samaria*, 51.

38. Becking, *Fall of Samaria*, 74–75; Stephanie Dalley and J. N. Postgate, *The Tablets from Fort Shalmaneser* (London: British School of Archaeology in Iraq, 1984), 169, 177.

39. Becking, *Fall of Samaria*, 74–75.

40. Joseph W. Swain, *The Ancient World* (New York: 1950), 1:179–80; A. T. Olmstead, *History of Assyria* (Chicago: University of Chicago Press, 1960), 646–55.

41. Oded, *Mass Deportations*, 22–25, 46–47, 77, 84–86.

42. Oded, *Mass Deportations*, 35–38.

43. Becking, *Fall of Samaria*, 70–71; Oded, *Mass Deportations*, 63–64.

44. 2 Kings 19:11–12.

45. Geoffrey W. Bromiley, ed., *The International Standard Encyclopedia* (Grand Rapids, Mich.: William B. Eerdmans Publishing Co., 1982), 613–14.

46. Oded, *Mass Deportations*, 81–84, 89–91.

47. Annie Caubet, *Khorasbad le Palais de Sargon II, Roi d'Assyrie* (Paris: Le Documentation francaise, 1995), 54.

48. Caubet, *Khorasbad le Palais de Sargon II*, 66–68.

49. *The Septuagint Version of the Old Testament and Apocrypha* (London: Zondervan Publishing House, 1976), 23.

50. *Septuagint Version*, 24.

51. *Septuagint Version*, 34.

52. *Septuagint Version*, 23.

53. John L. McKenzie, *Dictionary of the Bible* (Milwaukee: Bruce Publishing Co., 1965), 333.

54. Metzger, *Apocrypha of the Old Testament*, 65 (2 Esdras 13:41–45).

55. 1 Nephi 22:4.

56. 3 Nephi 15:15, 17:4.

57. Matthew 15:24.

58. Matthew 10:5–6.

59. 3 Nephi 17:4.

60. Exodus 19:5–6.

61. Joseph Smith Jr., *History of The Church of Jesus Christ of Latter-Day Saints,* ed. B. H. Roberts, rev. ed. (Salt Lake City: Deseret Book Company, 1951), 1:315.

62. Doctrine and Covenants 133:28–29.

63. Doctrine and Covenants 133:21–24.

64. Revelation 7:4, 14:1; Doctrine and Covenants 77:11.

65. Doctrine and Covenants 77:11.

66. Doctrine and Covenants 133:32–34, 17–18.

67. Genesis 1:9.

68. Doctrine and Covenants 133:23–24.

69. Doctrine and Covenants 133:26–27.

70. 1 Peter 3:18–19.

71. Matthew 12:40.

72. Doctrine and Covenants 133:26–27.

73. Genesis 1:9; 8:2–3.

ABOUT THE AUTHOR

Clay McConkie is a native of Utah. He has taught in the Salt Lake City Schools for thirty years.

He received a B.A. degree in history from Brigham Young University and an M.S. and Ph.D. in education from the University of Utah. He and his wife reside in Provo, Utah, and are the parents of four children.

In connection with military service and church missions he has traveled in the European area, being especially interested in cultures pertaining to ancient Greece and Rome. This partly explains his interest in the concept of the lost tribes.

Another book by the author on this same topic is *The Gathering of the Waters, A New Discussion of the Lost Tribes of Israel.*